SAAMA
INNOCENTS IN ASIA

Jonathan Falla

Stupor Mundi

2018

First published 2018 by Stupor Mundi Books

Scotland, UK.

www.stupormundibooks.wordpress.com

mundibooks@gmail.com

Set in Garamond MT 11 pt

Stupor Mundi was the name often given to the Holy Roman Emperor Frederick II of Hohenstaufen (d.1250). A man of great talents and learning, he was a lawgiver, patron of the arts and sciences, linguist and warrior whose Sixth Crusade retook Jerusalem by negotiation rather than bloodshed. His court at Palermo was described by Dante as 'the birthplace of Italian poetry.'

The author

Jonathan Falla was born in Jamaica in 1954, and took his degree at Gonville & Caius College, Cambridge. Trained later as a nurse, he worked for aid and disaster relief agencies including Oxfam, Save the Children, and Health Unlimited, before returning to paediatrics in the UK. His published writing includes five novels, history, ethnography, poetry in translation, and essays, and he is the author of award-winning feature film and drama. He is now a lecturer in the arts for the Open University and for St Andrews University, and is Director of the St Andrews Creative Writing Summer School.

Awards have included Best Film, 'Most Promising Playwright', a Fulbright Senior Fellowship at USC Los Angeles, a PEN fiction prize and a Creative Scotland Award.

He lives with his family in Scotland where he is a serving member of the Children's Panel.

Fiction by Jonathan Falla
Blue Poppies
Poor Mercy
Glenfarron
The Physician of Sanlúcar
The White Porcupine
The Morena & other stories
Terraferma & other stories

Non-fiction
The Craft of Fiction: how to become a novelist
True Love & Bartholomew: rebels on the Burmese border
Ramón López Velarde: 21 Poems (translations)
The Luck of the Devil: memoirs of Robert Le Page
Hall in the Heart: a Fife parish hall and its community
Beyond the Roadblocks: squibs & longshots 1984-2015

Drama
Topokana Martyrs Day
Free Rope
Down the Tubes
River of Dreams
The Hummingbird Tree

CONTENTS

PREAMBLE

> I dare boldly say, that though I bestowed some time in writing the
> book, yet it cost me not half so much labour as this very preface. I
> very often took up my pen, and as often laid it down, and could
> not for my life think of anything to the purpose.
>
> *Don Quixote*

This is an account of a journey in 1974 from Istanbul to Kathmandu and
then to various destinations in India. It is also an autobiography; much of
my life found expression in the journey and the sharp education it
delivered, to a degree that startles me as I write about it several decades
later. It is in a small way an historical document of the old 'hippy trail to
the East' which came to an end in 1979. And it is a love story – and it
makes me melancholy to see even from this beginning that the relationship
could not have endured common life.

Reconstructing the bare facts of the journey was easy, although after
nearly forty years I no longer have a continual memory of events, only
flashes and glimpses: a muddy pathway, the interior of a room, the view
from a window, someone touching my arm. It is as though I am seeing
things from the corner of my eye. I kept a diary which provides both the
narrative outline and little hooks with which to retrieve textures, colours,
sounds, emotions.

The links began to snap and the memories to distort, however,
immediately on my return. At my mother's cottage in Oxfordshire, I
attempted to recreate the tea I had been drinking all across India, the dust
leaf and milk boiled together with ample quantities of sugar. Only days
before, I had been consuming pints of this, but now it was quite revolting.

In the next four decades, material things were lost. Of all the fabrics I
bought, I have today just one: the cheapest, roughest horsehair blanket,
which is draped over the back of my study couch even now. But where is
the peculiar Afghan knife Georgia bought for me? And the Iranian bird
talisman? I still have the sitar and the flutes, but not the little talisman.

I find that I do not even have the original diaries. Some time after my return, I typed the two notebooks neatly onto A4 paper, gave it a title and had it bound like a university thesis, including photocopies of the handful of drawings. But I seem to have disposed of the original notebooks. Why did I do that? I've lost that direct link forever, and I cannot be sure that what I wrote on the day has been retold faithfully. Any amount of editing, conscious and unconscious, may have intervened, though I no longer know where. Indeed, obvious lies have crept in, because in the retyping I bolstered my self-image as a student of high literature; I quote one poem not published until after my return, and another from a book which – I now see from the flyleaf – was given me for my birthday a year later.

The one advantage of a four decade gap is that I no longer feel the humiliations of 1974, and don't much care who witnesses them.

I have an album of photographs from the journey, the black-&-white prints glued into a cheap children's scrapbook; on the cover, a water-rat dressed in waistcoat and boots is fishing. The paper is coarse, its colours now badly faded. To assemble my illustrations I had to ease the old photos off the sugar-paper with a fish slice, leaving spaces much darker than the surrounding page. In doing so I weakened another link with the immediate memory, the album I had made within a few weeks of my return. I shall return the photos to the album soon but it will not be the same. Identical, but not the same.

And when I look at the drawings, I find something odd: most of these are sketches made from life, but some are not; they are drawings copied from photographs. I know this because I have found the photographs. At some stage I must have thought it preferable, more convincing or more appealing to increase the number of drawings in the diary, and so I took certain photographs and carefully re-drew them as 'life sketches'. Probably it is obvious which ones these are.

I have revisited our various destinations on Google Earth, that illusory system that suggests that we are gazing down in real time (but which is in fact made up from aerial photographs of various ages), and which allows us to see almost – but not quite – into the lives below. I am amazed by the changes I find. In 1974, Pokhara in Nepal was a muddy village with one metalled street and something of a frontier atmosphere, the end of the Himalaya highway. Its mission hospital had a corrugated tin roof and one

British doctor; its hotels were mostly mud-walled 'lodges' without electricity or piped water or modern sanitation. Today, on Google Earth, Pokhara sprawls and is even described as a city; it has a modern teaching hospital and a college of nursing, a Hilton hotel, a 'spa resort', institutes of this and that. Along the shore of its lovely lake are scores of concrete residences; there are blue rowing boats for hire, their design vaguely Mediterranean; in 1974 there had been only dug-out canoes. All this change in four decades. Between me and present reality a wedge of time and activity has been inserted. I am no longer able to describe what you will find if you go to that place, only what once was. In the process of revisiting I am made older and out of date, a member of a previous generation. I don't object to this: the more archaic my experiences, the more authentic they seem. In fact, when I returned to India in person some twenty years after my first trip, it already seemed quite different, far more crowded and hostile.

This was (it has often been suggested) the Grand Tour of its day. The Journey to the East was part of a good education, with as much of an established itinerary as any followed by gentlemen of the 1770s. Just as the great age of the European Grand Tour was brought to an end by the Napoleonic wars, and was never quite the same thereafter, so too was the 'hippy trail' disrupted by the Iranian revolution and the Russian invasion of Afghanistan in 1979, by the Iran-Iraq war, and all the jihads and counter-jihads that have followed. There are now, however, nostalgia websites that recall the history of the trail. One discussion focuses on nothing more than memories of a certain scruffy hotel in Tehran. Some memoirists relate their entire journey, by 'Magic Bus' or train or car. A few do sense that they took part in something of marginal historical note. Some of the nostalgists make assertions that I don't recognise: some claim that the one and only object was to find as much cheap and excellent hash as possible, preferably consumed in its home setting among locals who went through life wearing an amused smile while sucking at hubble-bubbles. Drugs were never the object for me or for my two companions – nor, I think, for many that we met. I had little interest in drugs. I'd smoked a little here and there, and once took cocaine in a college toilet during a party, but I would not have dreamed of planning a long journey to seek it out. Besides, I would have been far too scared to go out into the streets of Tehran or Kabul or Kathmandu asking; I was keen to keep out of police stations. So were Georgia and Angela and, I think, most people on the road. In early 1974 the Turkish and Iranian governments had proposed to lift their bans on the cultivation of poppies, claiming that proper controls and the registration of producers of opium for medicinal purposes were preferable to a black market. But the Americans protested and blustered – and on the day that I crossed the border from Iran into Afghanistan, it was announced in Tehran that 239 people had been executed by firing squad over the last year for drugs offences, and that drug trafficking would remain a capital crime. No, I would not have dared.

So, why go at all? That summer I had intended to visit the USA, but the plan had fallen through. I was looking idly at a college notice board where a request for companions to the East caught my eye; it was haphazard. But for some people, the journey to India carried great personal significance and was long contemplated. Some travelled with paperbacks of Hermann Hesse's *Siddhartha*; some carried the Bhagavad Gita. Both my companions – Georgia, a school friend who had briefly studied Sanskrit at Cambridge, and Angela, an art student from London – had ideas of a quality of 'Indian-ness' that they sought. Both were inclined to moments of introspection and spirituality, though the stresses of the journey and our constant anxiety in the face of small difficulties now make the notion of seeking for eastern calm rather comical.

I was plain nosey – but a tad more than that. My university supervisor had commended to me a famous essay by the German sociologist Georg Simmel, published in 1911: *Das Abenteuer* (The Adventure). In this, Simmel describes the strange status that an adventure has in our being, something that happens on the periphery of our normal existence, and yet takes on a central importance in our lives; such an adventure may be a journey, or gambling, or a love affair. I brooded on this as I went; for all its inept, immature follies, my 1974 journey had great importance for me. Thereafter I became a publisher's editor in Java, and an aid worker in Uganda, Burma, Sudan and Nepal. I made a career writing drama and fiction derived in large part from observations such as I'd begun to collect on the hippy trail. I might have done none of this without a journey to the East. So I have little time for those snooty travel writers who look down their noses at scruffy youth blundering about the world, or who make sarcastic, derisive remarks about ignorant tourists. I was young, blundering, ill-informed, impatient, tactless and absurd in a hundred ways – and the experience shaped my life.

When I think of those nostalgia sites on the internet, I wonder: who are the people who now, several decades later, still day-dream about their journey? Have they settled down since? Why aren't they hard at work in their investment banks, workshops or laboratories? Why did they search the web for memories? Perhaps for them too something happened at the periphery of their lives which for a while took on a central importance.

Note: in 1974, the two cities were known to most English speakers as Benares and Bombay, not Varanasi and Mumbhai – and as this is a period piece I have left them that way.

Jonathan Falla, Cambridge 1974
Photograph by Patrick Reade

ONE

DON QUIXOTE IN ANATOLIA

These preparations being made, he found his designs ripe for action, and thought it a crime to deny himself any longer to the injured world.

Don Quixote

I took two books to the East. For the plane to Istanbul I had a copy of Djuna Barnes's *Nightwood,* much admired by T.S.Eliot. Georgia picked it up as we waited at Heathrow.

'Ooh, what's this?' she chirruped, and she began to read, taking it in with such efficiency that I was ashamed of my own slow reading, and of my notion that this thin book might be adequate for a whole plane journey.

'So much for that.' She had finished it before we even boarded the flight.

I recall not a word of *Nightwood.* I hated it before starting.

The other book was *Don Quixote.* It was a cheap American paperback edition, printed on poor paper that felt like the macerated wood it was made from, fibrous and discolouring at the edges. The print was small and so tightly packed onto the page that there was scarcely any margin, neither at the sides, top nor bottom; it was standing room only, the letters clinging to the pages by the tips of their serifs. It was like a ferryboat carrying an illegal throng of passengers: a capsize would kill preposterous numbers. On the back cover, the publisher's synopsis ended with this:

> To compound the comedy, Cervantes has his hero set out at midday – and the days in Spain can be really hot.

Throughout my journey I would peer at this statement, wondering why in all that wonderful story the midday heat had been highlighted.

But the piquant thing about this book was the binding. The eight-hundred or so pages were stuffed into a cover that was not big enough; the coarse paper had gradually swollen so that now it was like a corpse bulging out of its clothing. It was 'perfect bound', the pages held in by nothing

11

more than a smear of white glue down the spine, and this glue (old and cracking) wasn't up to the task; as I travelled, each page that I read detached itself. At first I tried to keep them together, stuffing them back between the covers. But the process was inexorable. However gingerly I turned the page, it would break free, as though the act of running my eye down the text unzipped the binding. Soon I gave up, and discarded each page as I read. So the litter bins along my route – in trains and railway waiting rooms, hotels and bus termini – each held a few pages of *Don Quixote,* and I imagined a story by Borges in which an obsessive bibliophile attempts to reconstruct the text of a lost masterpiece by retracing another reader's journey eastward, at each step hunting for the discarded pages of a book. The business of shedding pages had one advantage: as the days passed, *Don Quixote* became ever more emaciated and occupied less space in my bag.

However shabby the edition, it was a companion. The 1712 translation was that of Pierre Motteux – a French immigrant in London – a version which some still prefer today for its liveliness even if (as a later translator remarked), 'the flavour is distinctly Franco-cockney.' Motteux does have a bad name for inserting his own jokes, not that I'd have known which those were.

In July 1974 – just 262 years after Motteux published his *Quixote* translation in London, some 369 years after Part One of the original appeared in Madrid, and 399 years almost to the day since Cervantes was captured on his way home to Spain having battled the Turks at Lepanto, I flew into Istanbul where the airport Arrivals hall was a steel shed. Even at midnight it was thunderously hot, loud, disorienting, jostling and ungracious. We'd hardly started, and already we were tired and bad tempered, flapping at men who tweaked at and chattered at and pestered us with their taxis and their hotel cards. Angela, her great bulk intimidating the touts, swayed forward under her vast blue rucksack. We had that new journey instinct of constantly feeling for our bags, fearing that they'd be spirited off our shoulders for sale at a convenient rogues' night market just behind the customs shed. I recall the Opel taxi's broken-hearted seats, and sitting pressed up against Georgia's bony little flank, and realising just how close we would be for many weeks. I recall the drive through the steep cobbled back streets of the city, the usual altercation over the fare with bluster and counter-bluster:

'I shall take you to the police at once!'

'Good, you do that. Let us see what the police have to say!'

Until everyone has their bluff called or is too tired to bother. We were dumped in a cobbled lane that dropped steeply into a dangerous dark maze of alleys – a place where, after hours of hopeless wandering, one would surely collapse from exhaustion, and be dragged into cellars and tortured by sadists who didn't even speak English, prior to being weighted with old church brassware and dropped into the Bosporus from a skiff. But a few yards down there was a narrow doorway in a blank wall, and a night porter bleary behind a small desk. Angela – her person and her rucksack filling the narrow hallway – demanded loudly, impressively, to be shown to the roof.

'But we have rooms,' he returned, half-hearted.

Brilliant early sunshine, new and clean, woke me. On all sides, my companions huddled in their sleeping bags on the flat roof. I lifted my head over the parapet to look Hagia Sofia in the face, my first sight of the Orient. To my right was a sea of glistening oily grey, with ferries and tugs busying about. In the street directly below, a young man was setting out a barrow heaped with cherries of deep vermilion which he dashed with water from a tin mug to make them gleam, while up the cobbled hill came an older man pushing a cart with a brazier and urn to make a thick cardamom-scented coffee. He produced one for the cherry seller, which I thought I could smell from four floors above. There was a distant growl of traffic and occasional hoots from tugboats, but the clearest sound was the scrape of the coffee barrow's iron wheels on the cobbles, local and full of effort.

Wonderfully primitive, travel and travellers in 1974. We had no mobile phones, no recourse to internet cafes, no email with which to enquire about train travel beyond the next frontier, or to reassure our families or beg for a money transfer. We had no MP3 music in our pockets, not so much as a cassette player (the 'Walkman' had not yet been invented); no one then travelled wearing headphones, so perhaps we talked more and heard the world about us better, or perhaps not. No one possessed a synthetic fleece; we had woollen jerseys and cotton jackets. We had no 'trainers': they were new on the market then, and I wore the far more common desert boot, always smelling of plastic and hot cheap suede. My East German Praktika camera had no automatic metering, so I was obliged to wave a separate light meter at my subjects. We had no dread of AIDS of which we'd never heard; what everyone feared was hepatitis. We had very little money; we were poor students, and in Cambridge that spring I'd been in the habit of going to the bank each Monday morning to cash a cheque for £10 to see me through the week. In Tehran, in Kabul, in Kathmandu, we would count our money each day, spreading it out on hotel beds, wondering how little should be spent on dinner. We had no credit cards; we carried dollars in cash and travellers' cheques, buried in sweaty pouches worn at the waist next to the skin, but inclined to ride up until they sat across one's belly, with the damp passport and the carbon flimsies of the precious air tickets. No budget airlines in those days, only 'bucket shops' and what you could find in the darker recesses of Tarom or Egypt Air.

Our bags were very primitive. I had a rucksack made of bright orange nylon, not in the least waterproof. There were no plastic ladderlock fastenings then; my sack did not even have a strap and buckle. To secure the top flap, there were two nylon cords to be tied through chromed loops further down. There was no elastic to keep things snug, so I had everything in blue plastic freezer sacks. Someone at home had recommended lining one's rucksack with chicken wire to deter thieves from slitting it open, but I had baulked at that. The rucksack was strapped onto an external aluminium frame which rattled its tinny swivels in a cheap and embarrassing way. This frame had one considerable and unforeseen virtue: it was shaped like an L, and could stand upright unsupported. There was a six or seven inch gap between the foot of the L and the canvas sack strapped on above – and thus the sack would be clear of monsoon rain washing down an Indian street.

There is a sound maxim for travellers: take half the luggage and twice the money. Much of the space in my orange rucksack was taken up with a bulky sleeping bag, too many clothes, a large water bottle, and shoes. Forty-eight hours into the journey, I would willingly have abandoned most of it, had I not been too scared.

The other resource in short supply was information. There were no websites to search in 1974. We'd never heard of Lonely Planet or Rough Guides. All we had was Fodor's *India*, aimed at well-heeled Americans and recommending hotels that would have swallowed two months' budget in one dinner. Only later did we see something called the 'BIT Guide', stencilled foolscap sheets of notes for free spirits going East.

But we were not on our own; again and again, notice boards in certain hotels and coffee shops referred us onwards. So a handwritten card in the Pudding Shop in Istanbul would tell of a reliable ticket agent in Tehran; at a hotel in Herat, an Israeli girl would request company for the road to Kabul; a young Belgian in Kabul would commend a fairly safe bus service for the Khyber Pass – and we would gratefully follow his advice.

I recall almost nothing about Istanbul. Perhaps I was too excited or too pressed for time, but also too tired and too ignorant. Now that I'm grown up and have some idea of the Ottoman empire, I would be far more curious. But back then, when I was 20 years old, the Sublime Porte was just a door. I did not start writing my travel diary until we were in a train crossing Anatolia, so it has little to tell me of Istanbul. Now that I have read Ohran Pamuk's elegy to the burned wooden mansions of the Bosporus, now that I have studied art history and have some notion of domes and mosaics – now I would look more closely. I'd walk Constantine's walls, and track down impromptu music in bars. But at the time the little I knew of Turkey was tainted with puerile jokes about exquisite tortures (having one's testicles crushed between silk cushions) and an all-pervading homosexual sado-masochism.

All I remember of one of the most historic cities on earth is negotiating the crowds on the rising slope of Galata Bridge, also the nauseating smell of diesel at the back of a ferry, and the dusty staleness of the Blue Mosque which I was too tired to enjoy at all. I've read since that the overall blue tiling of that interior is 'somewhat monotonous', so perhaps my taste was better than I knew; I remember wanting nothing more than to lie down and close my eyes. What a waste of time travel can be.

I was absurdly prejudiced, and my expensive education had done little to dispel this; indeed, it was my education – mediated by the likes of Robert Byron, Kinglake, Buchan, and Lawrence, and bolstered by tales of torture and obscenity – that gave me the prejudice, since it had fed me all the reading required to build up a grotesque picture of the Turks who were the villains of a romantic tragedy stained by sordidness.

I've learned more since. I know now (from Runciman's account) of the fall of Constantinople in 1543, and the terrible hopelessness of the last emperor's plight:

> Constantine sent for his secretary Phrantzes and told him to make a census of all the men in the city, including monks, who were capable of bearing arms... Constantine was appalled by the figure... Against the Sultan's army of some eighty thousand and his hordes of irregulars, the great city, with its fourteen miles of walls, had to be defended by less than seven thousand men.

I know now that the besieging Turks held a great celebration in their camp, the fires, flares and torches being so bright that the desperate Greeks thought for a moment that the enemy camp was burning. And that the final assault, in the middle of the night, had at last overwhelmed the defenders lining the colossal walls – but only because someone had forgotten to close and lock a door, a little sally-port called the Kerkoporta, through which the Turks forced their entry.

And after the capture of the city, Sultan Mehmet had heard of the great beauty of a 14-year Greek boy, the son of Constantine's chief minister Lucas Notaras. He had given instructions that the boy be brought for his sexual pleasure. When Notaras had refused to give his son up to this fate, Mehmet had both of them decapitated, Notaras asking only that the boy die first, lest he should give in to being sodomised once his father was dead.

These are the sorts of things that I recall about Istanbul, not the place itself. But the scandalous atrocities during the sack of Constantinople by Christian crusaders in 1204 leave me indifferent. Why do I have trouble with Turkey? I'm not alone in this.

Not long after my visit the film *Midnight Express* appeared, the story of a young American jailed in Turkey for attempting to smuggle drugs through that same Istanbul airport. The distinguished production team gave way entirely to hatred, and Turkish prisons were shown as a Dantean purgatory of sado-masochism. *Lawrence of Arabia* stays in my mind partly for an image of Lawrence stretched across a bench in a small Ottoman garrison, being flogged by sweating, unshaven soldiers who leer with pleasure at his pain. The Turks themselves hardly helped; the film *Yol*, made a few years later, made an international impact, and in that story Turks bully each other with Ottoman relentlessness. The film's author, Yilmaz Güney, was himself infamous for chauvinism and physical violence towards women. It has all confirmed so many of my suspicions. How very lucky I am, with my university scholarship and my fellowships and my qualifications – and how very little good it does me in my attempts to think dispassionately.

I never asked my companions what they felt about Turkey; I would have been ashamed to discuss my prejudices, knowing that I was supposed to be intelligent. But no one wanted to linger there. We had no time for Turkey. We were rushing headlong to the East.

Among the photos lifted from my scrapbook is one labelled 'Leaving Istanbul'. Across a sandy foreshore is a strait of water beyond which, almost invisible in the grey haze, is a range of snow-capped mountains. In the bottom right corner, a boy is playing with two wheels on an axle taken from some small cart or pram. This is a view from the train window not long after leaving Haydarpasa on the Asian side of the strait, and we were travelling from right to left of this picture, heading East and looking south at the narrowing Sea of Marmara. The photo tells us that the day was hot, for the light and shadows are harsh. There is also a neat cement water fountain – a warning. As the train crept in all its exasperating slowness along the Marmara shore, inching towards Iran, I sensed an anxiety that I would have felt in hardly any other country.

My edginess waned a little as the train meandered across Anatolia; there was no hurrying the *Van Golu Ekspresi*. It was scheduled to take three days to reach Tehran from Istanbul, but that was a fantasy: five was likely. Had they told me the truth at Haydarpasa I would have fretted uncontrollably; we had so little time, we had to keep moving on, keeping to a schedule. But if we were in such a hurry, why not fly to India in the first place? Attaining Eastern calm was to be earned through experience and tests that Fate would set up for us – but Fate could be bloody irritating if it caused undue delay. Every morning we would examine our planning and try to estimate where we would be, and by which day, and whether the banks and borders would be open, or a certain bus running that evening.

When I am travelling, all is well as long as I am moving; if the bus stops I start to look round, wondering what is wrong. If the airport departures board doesn't change in its steady sequence, I pace up and down looking for signs of official activity. My own flight may not be due for another three hours, there may be no reason for the board to give new information: still, if none of the flights are leaving, I wonder if there are storms over the sea, or a civil war, or a universal systems crash. If my train stands still, I wonder if it has broken down, or if perhaps a bridge has been washed away, or if there has been a coup at an army barracks up the line.

One way or other I will surely have to turn around and start all over again, losing precious time and money, my plans unravelling… until, with no warning, the carriage jolts violently, we are going on, and I relax a little. However slowly the train crawls, as long as we are going forward, I can hope. So I tried to stop fretting on the *Van Golu Ekspresi*.

A gruff diesel dragged us further away from Istanbul up through citrus groves where often one could see boys. Usually there were two; one would be perhaps thirteen and his brother eight or nine years old. Always they walked with the elder brother leading and his loyal sibling trailing after. Always they wore lace-up shoes but no socks. In spite of the heat, both might be wearing woollen pullovers, sometimes sleeveless but still scarcely believable. Sometimes they'd be hauling a donkey with panniers, or a small sister, but older daughters were decently at home, what with all those strangers going past in trains, their forearms hanging limply out of the carriage windows to catch a cool breeze.

I began at last to enjoy the life: the getting off at each provincial station to souse my head under a tap on the platform; the foray into the buffet for

yoghurt; the stunned suspension of my yoghurt spoon halfway to my mouth as another gigantic Krupp steam engine coughed its way through: enormous black machines, thickly encrusted with pipes, domes, cow catchers, tubes, valves and levers.

You can see the cobblestone platforms, the huge sheds with pantiled roofs (nothing visible through the windows but one packing case in a far corner), and telegraph cables looping away into the distance. As the engines heaved backwards and forwards, I stood imagining an Ottoman scene seventy years before, complete with rolling stock bought from Germany at preferential rates in return for political humiliation. The station officials looked timeless, as did the small Turkish salary-men with their weary-looking suits and their fibreboard cases. But in my photograph there is a foreigner in a T-shirt, hair on his shoulders, shades over his eyes.

It seemed a very long way to the East, at this rate; we seemed to have adjusted to the speed of the countryside. Waiting beside the line were three huge ox-carts, heaped high with rough fodder. On top of each load there was clothing, tossed up there for safekeeping – but who owned the clothing? The only figure present was the usual young boy in a woollen hat. Who had built the carts? They were massive things constructed of timber – the wheels and axles too – all held together with wooden pegs and coarse hemp cording. The provenance of the heavy loads of fodder was a mystery, for there was nothing growing here except short tussocky grass. And their destination was strange too, for there were no farms to be seen, only a railway shed. Where did the boy live? He made me think of the poor peasantry who formed the Ottoman army – Little Mehmet, as Tommy Atkins was known in Turkey – the illiterates who were reputedly handcuffed to their own machine guns at Gallipoli.

The reason for the train making such slow progress was that it kept stopping to pick up hitch-hikers. On the bare Anatolian heights, when the curves of the railway allowed, one could see them miles ahead, waiting patiently. In my photo there are six tiny figures, one a child, in a grassy landscape without trees, or fields, any visible animals or human dwellings. The 'express' train has halted; two carriage doors hang open above the

stone ballast. From the carriage windows, the forearms dangle. In a second photo, a passenger has got so bored that he's climbed down beside the train to have a look. He wears an exotic tasselled shirt that belongs firmly in the 1970s. Those on board call: What's going on? Clearly, not much, although my scrapbook caption to this photo says: 'The Italian in the white hat tried to seduce Angela in Tehran.'

Travel websites used to show the old *Van Golu Ekspresi* with a warning that 'this is not the most comfortable of trains.' In more modern versions, the carriages have a trim white livery striped with red and blue, and smart air-conditioned couchettes. My 1974 photos show battered dark green rolling stock with compartments of stiffly upright leatherette upholstery – which I recall was dark green also – and with ashtrays made of a dull grey alloy (giving off a sour, dirty smell), also little brass chains to hold the sliding inner doors shut so that one could not be robbed at night. The passengers are unsmiling; they shift and wriggle and gaze out listlessly. Standing to dangle one's wrists out of the window was preferable.

In the compartment together with my companions Angela and Georgia, there was Farooq, an Iranian economics student, and Erik, a Norwegian studying medicine who had attached himself to us at Istanbul airport, had followed us to the roof of the hotel, and now the train. For hours on end, Georgia sat with her fingers in the pages of a book as though about to read, or would stand at the window with the sweat highlighting the scapulae under her thin cotton print, a flowery, high-waisted thing that emphasised her small breasts and her thin legs that seemed overlong for her body. Angela would gaze wistfully out of the window, then find her airmail pad, perch it on her ample knee and cover the paper with forceful ballpoint scribble to her boyfriend in London.

From time to time, Farooq and Erik would start a little chatter, Farooq asking why his breath smelled and what advice could the doctor give, please? In my photo of Farooq he looks friendly, with his mouth open and slightly twisted, as if sniffing doubtfully at his own odours.

We passed through Ankara in the early morning, but were perhaps asleep. On we trundled, across Galatia province and into Cappadocia, higher and higher, through towns whose names meant nothing to me; if I was to take at random the names of a dozen cities in Italy, France, Germany or Spain I would recognise almost every one, but not Eskisehir, Irmak, Kayseri, Sivas, Yolçati, Elazig and Mus. These were significant destinations for the *Van Golu Ekspresi*. Some places, dignified into importance on the Turkish State Railways map, were in reality only a junction: Bogazköprü, Çentinkaya. The latter was important because there one could choose whether to ride to Erzincan or Malatya. At this stage, after Sivas, line construction must have been ever more arduous, winding through mountain valleys approaching Kurdish territory. To the north and east, the Ottomans and Russians had been slugging out their frontier differences since the early 1800s.

We were now high up; less than one hundred miles to the north was Erzurum, scene of the extraordinary final chapter of Buchan's *Greenmantle* in which, in early 1915, the Russian cavalry sweep down upon the Turks like the horsemen of the Apocalypse. Baking in our train, I strained to imagine the blizzards that bury these mountains each winter; foreigners go to Turkey in the summer and seldom see the snows, only the bare hills. In December 1914, the Turkish army mustered near the town of Sarikamiş to keep the Russians out of Erzurum. The Turkish IX Corps, attempting to outflank the Russians, set out along a mountain ridge at 8,000 feet. Many of the soldiers did not possess overcoats, and there was supposed to be complete secrecy, so cooking fires were forbidden – not that there was anything to burn or to cook; they had nothing but bread and olives. Storms began, driving snow and ice into their faces; the temperature plunged far below freezing. By 26th December, long before they made contact with the Russians, the 23,000 men of IX Corps were reduced to 10,000; the rest lay dead in the drifts. After this, exhausted, famished and frostbitten, Little Mehmet had to fight a protracted battle; three weeks later, the remaining two hundred officers and one thousand men of IX Corps surrendered to the Russians. The Turkish commanders had even less notion of Cappadocia in the snow than I.

Snow pervades the Turkish experience in ways I scarcely imagine. In Istanbul – Ohran Pamuk tells us – it snows just a few days each year, but the snowfall possesses the city, and the novelist's imagination is quite taken over by it. In that brutally fine film, *Yol*, a husband leaves prison to find that his wife has resorted to prostitution; he carries her on his back through the winter snows to her punishment, only to have her freeze to death; he relents towards her too late. So the thought of snow has me relent towards Turkey. I think of the little people standing by the line hoping the *Ekspresi* will stop, precisely the poor peasants whose men would be conscripted by the Turkish army. Do they stand there in the winter too? I think of Little Mehmet stumbling up the ridge above Sarikamiş. I think of the boys I'd seen trudging with their brothers through the citrus groves near Istanbul; they'd have been conscripts in 1914, and half of them probably named Mehmet, after the Sultan who triumphed over Christian Constantinople in 1453.

But as we passed by in our long slow express, Little Mehmet's commanders had something else on their minds: they were mustering their men on the south coast of Turkey for the invasion of Cyprus two weeks later.

When the train reached the middle of nowhere, there was the lake, Van Golu, ringed with beige hills and with a steamer patient at the jetty. A small black shunting engine puffed and hissed, laboriously dismantling the train and tucking it on board carriage by carriage, like the old boat train from London to Paris. The passengers sat on a stack of sleepers watching the slow manoeuvre, not daring to doze in the sun or to walk anywhere in case the operation concluded quickly; perhaps they only took half the carriages from here. The ship might disappear over the long lake towards Iran, leaving some poor traveller in the centre of treeless Anatolia with his bags gone east and not a yoghurt to his name.

Today, only the luggage van is taken on the ship; an Iranian train meets it at the other side of Lake Van, still well within Turkey. That they bother shipping the train at all tells us that the high, remote landscape was a dreadful place for building railways. This bleak region was as far as the Russians had driven into Turkey in 1914. Perhaps they'd thought about going further, looked at the hillscape, and wondered what was the point.

In Edinburgh there used to be a Lake Van Armenian Monastery in Exile Restaurant, housed in a gloomy redbrick Victorian building near Holyrood palace, with no external signage at all. My sister and I dined in a gloomy room lined with sepia portraits of martyrs of Armenian nationalism, and of the abbots of a monastery that had stood on an island in the lake. The chef – a monk – sat with us between courses to lecture us on the injustices suffered by Armenians in Turkey. At the end, he turned on a cassette player and obliged us to join him in a folk dance. This is all I know of Lake Van and its monastery, although I can say: I've been there. It was night when we crossed on our boat.

At dawn, the train stopped at the Iranian border. Nothing happened. We wandered, lethargic and just a little worried, because we had been groomed by a smuggler and talked into carrying goods. He was a Tehrani, a jolly young man with a tousled mop of hair. At Istanbul he had loaded onto the train four huge suitcases of flash Italian-style clothes, and surely Customs somewhere would jump on him. So he went along the train seeking out Europeans, persuading each person to carry a pair of trousers, a suit or a shirt. Half of the passengers in the couchettes must have been complicit.

For five hours, nothing happened; we sat and waited. Georgia's nerves were frayed; she snapped if spoken to, and said repeatedly that we were fools, but did nothing to discard the designer jeans she'd accepted from the smuggler. Opposite her, Angela sat mountainous and silent, staring at her still unfinished letter to London. Farooq the economics student and Erik the young doctor debated halitosis. Precious time passed.

Suddenly, Iranian Customs were upon us, a charming young man. He touched my orange rucksack as though in blessing, grinned, said a few words in Farsi and vanished. Farooq laughed.

'He's a third-year student at Tabriz University, just doing it as a holiday job. I thought there would be many soldiers.'

The smuggler was thrilled, rushing up and down the carriage gathering up his trousers, buying everyone kebabs and beers from the dining car, and singing Persian love songs.

We had not escaped the passport men, however; they had boarded the train. I was squatting peaceably in the toilet when the locked door began to open. A uniformed figure with a master-key tried to join me, bawling 'Pusspor! Pusspor!' I kicked the door shut and relocked it, and he went away.

TWO

PLACING TRUST IN IRAN

> In the adventure, we proceed on the hovering chance, on fate...
> We risk all, burn our bridges and step into the mist as if the road
> will lead us on no matter what. This is the typical fatalism of the
> adventurer. The obscurities of fate are no more transparent to him
> than to others, but he proceeds as if they were.
>
> *Georg Simmel*

As the train crawled in through Tehran's suburbs, the passengers once again dangled their wrists out of the windows and stared, and the city children threw stones at them.

There were well-known staging posts on the route to India. In Istanbul there had been the Pudding Shop where (nostalgia websites now tell me) one 'picked up a chick' as a travelling companion (the site postings are all from men). There were others ahead. One felt obliged to visit; they were checkpoints, peopled by young travellers embarrassed to be homesick, who would eat the carrot cakes and fruit crumbles made especially for this clientèle, and would rummage through discarded paperbacks: Wilbur Smith in a German translation; a handbook to Central Asian birds minus its cover. But first they would peer at the notice boards hoping for some item of information concerning exchange rates, or hotels, or companionship or rescue of unspecified sorts that would enable them to achieve that elusive state of calm they were not yet finding as they worked their way East.

In Tehran, one stayed at the Amir Kabir hotel – gone now; after the 1979 revolution it was shut down, being a nest of foreign degenerates. It occupied two upper floors of a curious building vaguely resembling a 1930s petrol station or a Handley Page of Imperial Airways, with a curved prow and two high wings over a drab and busy street; below the hotel, the horseshoe-shaped yard was a tyre shop, and the enclosed acoustic rang all day with the dropping of steel rims and dinging of tools, and reeked of hot rubber. It was said that the Amir Kabir's proprietor took charge of one's

29

passport because otherwise guests would jump from the first floor balconies down onto the heaps of tyres, to make a getaway without settling their bill. I imagined men with tyre levers and rubber solution looking the other way as bill-defaulters rained down in the early morning. The nostalgia websites recall a hotel diet of fried egg and chips.

From our window – in a concrete façade painted with white lines to evoke ashlar masonry – one could survey see a main street of dour shops, Simca and Opel cars, double-decker buses, and in the distance the domes and minarets of a large mosque. A blurred snap of the interior of our room shows steel cots packed in, and my primitive rucksack on its aluminium frame. On my bed are personal things: a notebook, a Bartholomew map, a plastic treble recorder in three sections. We were endlessly unpacking and repacking, anxious not to lose track of something (we did not know which item it would turn out to be) that might be the key to survival. The gloss paint on the wall, up to dado level, is so shiny as to clearly reflect the steel bedsteads. There is a fuzzy Air India poster curling off the plaster, a washbasin in a far corner and, mounted on the wall, an improbable telephone, the old black variety with a dialling spinner and a plaited fabric-covered cord. On the furthest cot lies a figure with bare feet projecting from a thin dress and a towel round her head, reading: that is Georgia. Another of her dresses – pale cream, with embroidered borders and her usual high waist – hangs limp on a wooden stand; I can smell the faint sweet sweatiness that must have hung about us. What did decent Iranians think of three of us piled into one room? There were brief thunderstorms – the first at this time of year for more than a decade, said Farooq. They were like nasty hints.

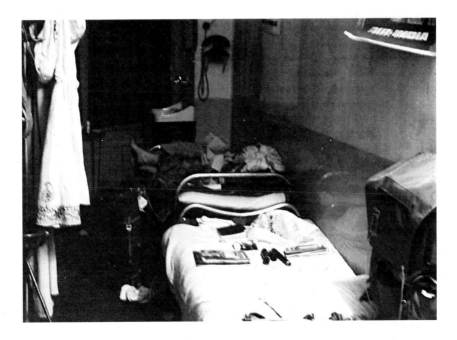

Erik the Norwegian was to work with rural health programmes as part of his medical training. Farooq invited him to stay with his family. Farooq had a tendency to pronouncements of unimpeachable rectitude:

'We must make our country better for the working man. We must do many things, but we must take our time.' He was, however, rather cagier about discussing what was actually wrong with the country.

We walked Tehran in a V formation, with me at the centre and slightly to the rear of Georgia and Angela, flapping to keep curious hands off the girls' bottoms, Angela incredulous at their impertinence, Georgia nervous. Men closed in on us. A student of English stopped me in the street and asked me to explain the difference between two past conditional sentences which he showed me in his exercise book. Then he offered me cash for a night with Angela. She was big, and they seemed to like them big.

I disliked Tehran immediately for its heat, its shabby cement buildings, and its ill-maintained double-decker buses (painted blue) pumping out diesel exhaust. One was supposed to buy a ticket before boarding, but I did not know that and was volubly shouted at in Farsi; I smiled sweetly and nodded until they lost interest. Whole streets sold one item only: tyres, carpets, hats, more tyres and more carpets. The Shah gazed down on his people from a thousand framed portraits; in the carpet shops one could buy gaudy tapestry versions of the portraits, at once benign but stern, and woolly. It would surely be a capital offence to place those on the floor.

And here was a bazaar – the first that I had ever set eyes on – deep caverns with thousands of plastic shoes racked up high, with cages like prison cells for songbirds, with cosmetics, synthetics and plastic baubles in dayglow pink and orange. The tunnels, lit by strings of coloured lights, zigzagged under the vaulted roof of the hot, dark arcades.

Half the day we were trying to keep up momentum, to keep moving, organising, walking, seeing, experiencing the Orient, 'travelling'. But the heat claimed every second hour. On the steel cots of the Amir Kabir Hotel, a cross-section of Western youth lay in various degrees of heat exhaustion and debility, visible through the bedroom doors propped open for any slight draft of air. In the travel agencies and ice-cream parlours they lingered, assessing their chances of making it to the East. I met in a bus office a student boy from Belfast who had got as far as Kabul before being

32

hit by dysentery and giving up. Angela liked to take all her medicines (provided by her doctor boyfriend) out of her rucksack, lay them on her cot and gaze at them fondly. Conversation between the many foreigners in the hotel was a protracted exchange of opinion on the control of dysentery and the avoidance of hepatitis. I realised that the carbon flimsies of my Egypt Air ticket home from Bombay were my best insurance that I would reach India, that flight being the quickest way home.

How unnecessarily difficult I make it all sound, but there was a notice board in the Amir Kabir covered with pleas and warnings:

– Canadians! Change your traveller's cheques before Herat!
– Avoid Kandahar Restaurant in Kabul: we saw the kitchen.
– Hasn't anybody got anything for me to read?
– Two Welsh girls seek a male companion to escort them
    back to Istanbul. We can't stand any more hassles.

Did young gentlemen on the Grand Tour *circa* 1780 feel beset by touts, pickpockets and dysentery, find themselves short of reading matter, and unable to stand any more hassles? They'd have had their tutor and a factotum to sort things out, but not every tutor can have been competent and not every factotum scrupulous. His young Lordship may have

33

wondered what he was getting into. Would he make it over the Alps? Would he find a passable bed, lose his letters of credit, or be swindled out of his last Maria-Theresa dollar? Did he unpack and repack as sedulously as Angela? Were there notice boards at the inns on the Appian Way? They must have exchanged jittery information somehow.

So, two hundred years later, we did not open ourselves to the East, but drew together defensively on our cots in our room over the tyre repair shop.

After one night at Farooq's house, Erik returned to the Amir Kabir. The Shah (who smiled so benignly down from the tapestries) had sent his secret police – the SAVAK – to look for Erik and to check his credentials. Farooq's family were terrified and had asked Erik to leave at once.

All this had Angela in a stir. She had spent much of the train journey composing letters to her man in London, but in Tehran asked me, very cagily, what I thought about having love affairs on holiday while you had someone else at home. Perhaps recalling Georg Simmel, I replied breezily that maybe it was all part of the adventure. It now appeared that the explanation was Erik, with whom Angela could be found skulking in our room, and who spent the night on our floor after fleeing the SAVAK.

That same evening, the Italian with the white hat tried to lure her off to the classier Baghdad Hotel for a night of passion. Angela had a pretty, freckly face fringed by long fair hair, though she was very fat. This never discouraged anyone.

We went to buy tickets to Meshed, as far East as the train could take us. After an hour of scrambling on and off buses to find the station, an hour and a half of standing in the wrong queue out of doors, then another wrong queue, there came the realisation that we had no language in common with the ticket clerk. A friendly student intervened, buying us our tickets for Meshed. This was to have consequences.

We retreated to a cafe, crowded but cooler than the street. I approached the counter; another handsome student came to serve us. He

34

saw the two girls and, for a change, was more taken with the slight, diffident, red-haired figure of Georgia a few feet away, and he gave me a broad grin.

'Oh yes! She is yours?'

I returned a smile and a non-committal wave of the head. He was entranced by Georgia.

'Oh, she is wonderful. The hair! She is good? She is very good?'

'She is wonderful,' I agreed.

'She is wonderful! I give you tea half-price.'

Which perhaps he did, though I couldn't read the price list so who knows. Georgia detected the conversation and flushed angrily.

In this mildly cosmopolitan cafe was a scattering of young Iranian women in Western dress, drinking coffee in public, beneficiaries of the Shah's White Revolution that so offended his other subjects. Outside, almost all women were in full black shrouds. They intrigued and piqued me; what was under all those wraps? In my diary, I quote this:

> I could easily turn traitor to measly Hellas
>
> For any one of thirty
>
> Argent and gleaming
>
> Iranian damsels.

Although, as *The Elegies of Quintilius* were not published until the following year, I must have typed it in later.

I loathed the city, its stink and oppressive climate. I met an American girl who was working as a PA; she'd been there two years and so despised Tehran that she could not understand why she stayed. Then she admitted that she earned a small fortune each month.

It took seven hours to reach Isfahan. The bus had air-conditioning, a toilet, free sweets, iced water and cola, but the frilly curtains hanging in rich swags with tassels hurt my ear if I tried to sleep resting my head against the window. By my side, Georgia nodded uncomfortably.

Outside, the high grass prairie of eastern Turkey was long gone; Iran looked like another planet, the gaudy world of Sci-fi novels. Ragged windsills were painted crimson, purple, or Burnt Sienna. Huge, sweeping multicoloured rock formations in the mid-distance appeared to shiver in the heat, a technicolor ripple of strata across the desert. There was an inhospitable salt lake, a great shallow dish of turquoise edged with crusty white. Otherwise, just a vast dusty stillness; only occasionally was there a spring with a flurry of vegetation, a delicate cluster of mud buildings looking incomprehensibly content to be there surrounded by all that ferocity. What might it have been like, to be the first human arriving in such a place? I imagined coming there with my family and a small string of mules carrying my belongings, fleeing some war, finding ourselves at one of those tiny oases and deciding to stop. How long could one peer at the vast surrounding landscape, knowing nothing of what lay beyond the endless coloured rock ripples? Even snug in an oasis, how could one tolerate the ignorance, the exposure, the defencelessness?

The turn of a rock spur revealed an enormous wire-bound army camp.

I realised that we were racing; there was another bus alongside us. Flocks of identical Mercedes buses ran this route south to Isfahan, with little to choose between them for decor or speed. Across the flats they competed, two vehicles side by side for mile on mile, with more behind. If a cloud of dust in the distance turned out to be two buses coming in the opposite direction, drivers would take to the rough ground. Wrecks littered the desert.

Georgia and Angela sat on a shady Isfahan street corner while I enquired after a hotel. I entered an airline office where a smart young man leaned across the counter to chat up the lady clerk.

He looked me over.

'Are you many?'

'I've two friends.'

'Boys or girls?'

'Two girls.'

'I can help you. I have travelled; I know it is very difficult when you have little money. People try to take it from you and always you are tired, very tired.'

The airline clerk agreed that most people were lice.

'So,' the man continued, 'we must help you. I will give you my garden summerhouse free for three nights. How about that?'

'They will like your summerhouse,' said the clerk. 'Everyone does.'

'You will like it. It is new, it is very clean. My name is Hassan, and we will see all of Isfahan together.'

That year, for my birthday, my sister had given me a 1912 edition of the Rubaiyat of Omar Khayam, with pleasing 'photogravures after drawings' of Persian gardens. Lady Evelyn Sykes (wife of British consul Sir Percy Sykes c.1910) hardly ever stepped outside her safe and lovely Persian garden, not in eight years residence. Such thoughts (or merely the idea of all the money saved) may have gone to my trusting head.

It was indeed a new summerhouse in a walled garden on the edge of town, in the Persian tradition. There were apricot and pomegranate trees, and water tanks with lilies clamped shut against the late afternoon sun. Georgia and Angela looked about warily, saying a few mutedly nice things, weary and apprehensive.

Hassan pulled our rucksacks out of his Volkswagen and pushed them through the front door.

'It's not finished yet.' He tweaked at loose wires sticking out of the plaster like tendons out of butchered flesh. 'But it's clean. You can sleep in any room you wish. There is no light inside yet but there are lights in the garden so you can see. But you leave your bags now. We will go into town. We will have dinner and then I will show you things. Tomorrow we will drive everywhere. We shall have a very nice time. I shall introduce you to Isfahan.'

We wanted only food and sleep. Packed into the VW we drove back into town turning suddenly into a vast floodlit arena where a multifaceted blue shimmer hazed my sore eyes: the Maidan-i-Shah and the mosques, gloriously lit up.

In an expensive and empty restaurant, the girls retreated into tense silence. We ate kebabs and rice, yoghurt and leaves with a taste somewhere between sorrel and mint. There was nothing for it but to enjoy the food, to talk and ask questions to which Hassan responded in an increasingly abstracted manner, giving quick glances at the sullen girls who had given up eating. The waiters stood immobile, watching from a distance.

Then Hassan wanted to take us on somewhere for a drink but the girls insisted that it was time they slept. He drove us back to the summerhouse now lit only by the outside lamps, baleful moons on stalks leering over the rose bushes. Georgia and I went inside and began spreading out sleeping bags while Hassan declared his hand with Angela, sitting with her on the summerhouse steps by the open door of the VW.

'You I can love. Those two will sleep together, we two will sleep together. Why not?'

We could hear all this clearly. Georgia, her small mouth pursed tight, did not so much as look at me.

Angela had not the venom to swear at Hassan, or was scared that we'd be out on the streets. She tried to both refuse and be friendly, explaining that she was spoken for at home. The muttered supplications and fencing went on for twenty minutes; Georgia continued to arrange our bedding, then told me that I should intervene.

Hassan left, but with a parting shot:

'I shall take you to your hotel tomorrow. I am flying to Rome.'

The girls slept little, convinced that he would climb in through the window at midnight. We lay in a tightly packed defensive row, thrilled. Hassan came at 7 a.m., put us in his Volkswagen and dumped us at a roundabout. I wonder now at my astonishing gullibility; you might think that an expensively educated twenty-year-old would have learnt something.

This was Isfahan, and the Shah Abbas hotel was 3,000 *rials* a night; we could not afford to slip in for a fruit juice and to listen to the musicians in the foyer. At the Hotel Saadi, we pleaded poverty and got beds for 100 *rials* each. The sheets were clean, there was iced water, and we felt oddly guilty: this was hardly roughing it to the East.

Most things in the hotel were painted purple.

Out and about, haggling over textiles in the bazaar, we watched each other's performance critically. Angela wrestled R1,200 down to R400 for a fragment of '800-year-old' block-printed cotton which looked like something snipped off Granny's apron. Georgia managed R800 down to R500. It seemed to be a gauge of our ability to cope. Why was I buying a scrap of tatty printed cotton at all? It was because it had little birds on it, and because of a string of associations: my brother-in-law, a textile designer in London, had written a student dissertation on ancient *ikat* fabrics from the Yenesei River basin of Central Russia, and the soul-rider figures to be found on them; also, my Cambridge supervisor, Jeremy Prynne, had published a poem about Buriat shamanism in the Yenesei; and I had, at school, won a poetry competition for which the prize was a coffee-table book called *The Dawn of Civilisation*, including illustrations of those same fabrics from the Yenesei. As I work on this now, from the ceiling of my study hang the fringes of an *ikat* cloth that I bought in Indonesia five years after Iran; it is coloured deep grey-blues and oxide reds, and the design has soul-riders: reindeer-like animals (nothing of the sort exists in Indonesia) which carry the souls of the dead, represented by small birds, away to the afterlife. In the bazaar at Isfahan, I could dream that my scrap of printed fabric was a link to Asian deep history – although it was rather closer to the Rubaiyat than the Yenesei. It was quite pretty, predominately maroon, with roses and peacocks fit for a Persian garden, and pigeons fluttering in loose formation representing the lost souls of young travellers. It was badly patched, however, with a peculiar scrap of rose chintz plugging a tear. Unfortunately for my connection to either Omar Khayam or the shamans, I've long since lost it.

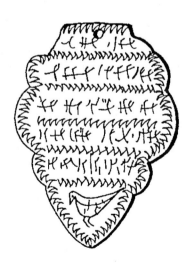

Another link with pre-historic Parthian pigeon-worship was the small talisman that I bought for a few coins, a sliver of thin incised silver, the design of which I copied into my diary.

In the Maidan-i-Shah, under the bazaar arcades, a merchant sat outside his brassware shop. He looked to have had a stroke; his face sagged on one side. A slow and gentle old man, he spoke heavy but courteous French, and invited us to join him for breakfast tomorrow. Our conversation with him was punctuated by huge, slow drops of rain beyond the arcades. Nearby we discovered pistachios, apricots, musk melon and ice put together in a blender for R8 a shot, and to hell with water purity.

In the morning the merchant awaited us on the arcade steps. We sat with him, looking out over the Maidan-i-Shah. The old man waved to someone in the shop; a boy emerged carrying an intricately wrought brass tray with cups of tea and a slab of yellow cake the size of a typewriter. The merchant contemplated this, murmured a blessing over it, then broke it into pieces for each of us, saying thickly:

'Vous êtes bienvenues en Persie.'

The Maidan-i-Shah was laid out in the 17th century as a polo pitch. I visualized Persian army officers galloping thunderously up and down this square, which seemed gloriously disrespectful and incongruous with the blue stillness of the mosques, the turquoise and lapis lazuli melting against an ultramarine sky, buildings without upper boundaries just as the best Gothic seeps into the English cloudrack. In those days I had notions of being a lyric poet, and wrote something beginning:

> Shah mosque-builder Abbas
> And many European cardinals and kings built
> To the end that the ends frayed...

I mislaid it, and that is as much as I can remember.

Robert Byron disliked what he considered the coarse tiling of the Masjid-i-Shah but to me it was coolly ravishing. Even the floors were blue, running into blue ponds in the open courtyards. One scarcely walked through such a building, but swam through it. At night they lit up the underside of the *ivans* – the great half-domes hung between two minarets like rugby goalposts – and then the dozens of little squinches in the underside of the *ivan* flickered between cold blue and warm gold, a jewelled honeycomb vulgarly supercharged to bring out the gasps of the tourists – but it was very striking. Robert Byron also disparaged the predilection of the authorities for petunia beds, even inside the mosques. But the old 'Friday Mosque' had tall arches of plain earth-coloured brick stepping away from me in diagonals into an ancient brown darkness, in tones and curves and surfaces of umber light, with the salts bleeding out through the pores of the brick and crystallising.

I bought a large yoghurt for R60 and it turned out to be solid cream with embedded pistachios. It was too much for me even to embark on. I gave it to the hotel porter who reappeared a few minutes later with a melon for us. And now we were all saying over enthusiastically how sweet and kind the Isfahani is, how easy he makes life for the foreigner. But the fact was, we never did feel 'bienvenues en Persie'; we felt that almost everyone except the old brassware merchant was out to get us. Perhaps that's what the British history in Persia deserved. In Isfahan, I began to think that no amount of architecture and historical sites on the road to India would matter one bit, if there wasn't cake for breakfast with a merchant under the arcades.

Also we were living too expensively, even when eating at the Isfahani version of a chippy. Over and again, we took everything out of our money belts, counted out the dollars and the traveller's cheques and divided it between the days ahead. It was not enough.

The porter woke us at 6 a.m. for the bus racing back to Tehran and straight onto the train for Meshed, onward without delay, leaving Erik to the SAVAK and the mosques.

'I can't believe you trusted him,' said Georgia, glaring round as though rank bad faith was visibly seeping from the Irani men in the train compartment.

'He didn't rip us off; he helped us buy tickets. What did you expect me to do? You don't speak any more Farsi than I...'

I swept the sweaty lank hair off my forehead. Angela hugged her big blue rucksack and said nothing, too sick, too nauseated, too infected, too pale and clammy for speech. She clung to the nylon, trusting nothing. I thought that she might faint and topple onto the gritty floor.

The inspector glowered in from the doorway and for the twentieth time waved the useless tickets at me. I sat straight and raised an ironic eyebrow; declaring the situation ironic made it a tad less terrifying.

My eye was fixed by Georgia, her face screened from the inspector by her straggling orange hair. She said to me mistrustfully:

'You're not going to let us down, are you?'

I felt hurt, unfairly blamed. I faced the inspector, and stonewalled in pointless English:

'We had an interpreter at Tehran station. He was a student, he misunderstood. It was not our mistake and we're not paying.'

I confirmed this with an emphatic crossing of my arms.

Georgia now refused to look at anyone, and returned to the *Journals of Anaïs Nin*. The official peered at her, suspecting her controlling influence. Standing behind him, three aggrieved passengers whose seats we had usurped touched his sleeve. The inspector turned and propelled them all away down the crowded corridor.

In our compartment, five Irani men travelled mostly in silence. A dark young labourer in a magenta corduroy waistcoat tapped Georgia on the arm and offered her something in a paper bag. But she shook her orange hair, shrilled, 'No, thank you!' and blocked the approach of the paper bag with the back of her bony hand. The five men regarded her a moment, but the hair and thin body were distasteful to them, and she was doing nothing to inspire sympathy. One man put a tatty fibreboard case on his knee and began to play cards with his neighbour opposite.

Night drew in tighter round the train. There was a mountain in silhouette – then it was gone. When we looked out at the plains of northern Persia, our own faces peered back at us from the black glass. Bolt upright, clattering and shaken, there was no sleep. Angela buried her miserable face into the top of the blue rucksack, the frame pressing into her fat thighs. Georgia read Anaïs Nin, as though putting herself into another world would settle the matter. Two of the labourers peeked over her shoulder.

The inspector returned with a policeman who hectored me in Farsi. I looked helplessly at Georgia who would not even meet my eye, blaming me for another débâcle The policeman could not make this pale, sour girl pay him attention. She declined to look at anyone; she read her book, and the policeman probably wanted to hit her. All three of us sat in surly defiance: one fat and sick, one greasy-haired and frightened, one skinny and insolent.

'Shouting at us in Persian won't help you,' snapped Georgia suddenly, still not looking up. I drew myself upright again and scrutinised the policeman as though the man were a poor actor auditioning. Aloofness was my best weapon until the policeman said, in any language:

'Passport!'

Drear-eyed, exhausted families sitting on suitcases in the corridor twisted their heads to peer at us through the scummy, scratched glass partition. The policeman and the inspector nodded in satisfaction as Angela at last raised her face; one passport came from the top pocket of her blue sack. Georgia, watched by the five labourers, tugged a pouch from under the dank cotton dress, up over her small, hot breasts. I was obliged to unbuckle my trouser belt to ease my sweat-stained, belly-rounded documents out through a zip.

The passports were thumbed and checked – as, again, were the bad tickets. The inspector produced a scrap of paper and wrote *280*; the policeman thrust this at me and pronounced in English:

'More you pay.'

'Two hundred and eighty *rials?*'

We looked sharply at each other – then, slowly, at the policeman. He wore a gun buttoned into a black leather holster. He wore black shoes, dulled with kicking students and other innocent people. He wore a short-sleeved shirt (his dark arms liberally black-haired), and he smirked like a bullying cat that drops a wounded mouse to watch it run. How we loathed him.

The policeman seemed to like the effect he had achieved, and said it again:

'More you pay.'

He was gratified to have the frightened boy and the thin girl speak at once, shaking little mouse-fists.

'It was not our fault! We were given the wrong tickets but we can't read them! Can't you get that into your head? We're not paying for others' mistakes. We're not paying!'

The policeman shrugged, tucked all three passports into the breast pocket of his shirt and turned away down the jolting corridor. The inspector watched him go, looked in once more at our dismay, then followed.

Georgia said to me: 'For God's sake, don't you dare pay it. They'll just split the proceeds.'

But the loss of the passports silenced us.

The lights stayed on all night; everyone's heads, reflected in the cold windowpane, sagged. We didn't talk, but retired into our private fears. The wheels hissed on curves like nerves on a lathe, and we ached to lie down. Three times, at remote hours, the policeman returned, pulled the passports from his shirt pocket and waved them – 'More you pay!' – and we ignored him. At which he'd shrug and pass along the train.

At noon next day the train slunk through the outskirts of the industrial city of Meshed, the end of the line, a place with a bus terminus, a shrine, a barracks and a bad reputation. The name means 'place of martyrdom'. From among shacks almost under the wheels, lovely doe-eyed children again flung pebbles at the carriages and the tired faces in the windows.

Disembarking, I saw the policeman stroll down the platform into a large office full of desks and more policemen. Georgia saw a station master gazing at her, and sent me to him. To my enormous relief, he spoke clear and careful English:

'In our country we begin the new day at 6 p.m. By our idea, you boarded a day late. Unfortunate only.'

It was clearly no one's fault and he, on behalf of Iran Railways, understood that. But he would not go to the police with us.

Angela found the toilets. She came out saying that they were alive with maggots and it made her puke – but a moment later she winced and went back inside. I saw that she was crying.

Georgia sat on a bench with our stupid, cumbersome packs: orange nylon, blue nylon, scarlet nylon, mine with a label depicting a backpacking bear in a Baden-Powell hat. I stood in front of her, and gazed dejectedly through the plate glass of the railway police office. She grew impatient.

'There must be a consul. Can't we find the consul?'

'There's nothing here but a barracks.'

'Two hundred and eighty *rials* – that's all our money for the bus! It goes at four, it's Friday and the banks shut at one, and we'll have to sit in Meshed until bloody Monday. We're losing time. I can't even walk around the streets, I'll get mauled by disgusting soldiers. I do not want to be here. We have to be moving, we don't have all year. How can we pay for a hotel with no money?'

'They might trust us.'

A silence, too painful. I looked towards the door of the toilets, noticing that the bottom edge of the wood was rotten.

'Is she really sick?'

'You mustn't pay.'

Angela came out; she had water splashed over her face, and smelled sour. The frayed hem of her floral cotton was soaked.

'This is so awful,' said Georgia.

We went into the police office, a blue-washed hall with oscillating fans screwed to the pillars and notices pasted to the whitewash. We sat on a bench and said it all again. No one paid us any attention. The policeman was seated at a desk some yards away, typing with one finger on a huge

46

machine that lashed the paper like a military whip. The three passports sat on his desk, disregarded. The railway police were clearing their desks to go home.

'It's Friday; everything closes,' I said. 'I have to pay.'

'I expect he'll arrest you for trying to bribe him, and then want a bribe to let us go.'

Angela spoke at last: 'I want to go to Afghanistan today.'

So we paid. The truth is that all these officials were doing their jobs perfectly properly.

We were given a receipt with our passports, in silence. We walked out under the crushing rucksacks, and came into a sun-bleached forecourt of gasping dust, with a palm garden rimmed in scalloped blue cement and litter. Beyond was a long road to the town, its banks closing just now. We stopped halfway across, staring straight ahead wordlessly, because we hated everything we saw, and didn't trust ourselves not to cry.

A modest car, none too new, swung at no great speed into the forecourt to our right. A male passenger got out, shook the driver's hand and disappeared into the booking hall.

We watched: in such a situation, such a car could not be trusted not to run us down. The car did in fact move towards us a little, and stopped again. The driver regarded us through the windscreen a moment, and then got out. He had grey hair and a neat moustache, but his clothes did not fit well. He had soft, blue eyes and a quiet voice. He said:

'Do you need help?'

Georgia said, 'No' and Angela said, 'I want to go to Afghanistan' and burst into tears. So I told him everything, repeatedly checking for Georgia's reaction. She regarded me with something like contempt, and the newcomer with resolute mistrust.

The man considered the tale: the closing banks, the lack of cash, the bus tickets we could not buy, the disaster. He remarked: 'You have left it late, but I have friend who manages a bank.'

With the rucksacks, the little car was jammed tight. We came to a two-storey cement building on a street corner, where the watchman was drawing a grille across the door. The driver got out and spoke to him, and the watchman tugged the grille back a foot, slipped inside and vanished upstairs. The blue-eyed man looked back at the car and smiled gently at us. We peered back through the small, grimy windows. Georgia murmured:

'This is absurd.'

'It's a bank.'

'How do you know? Tell me where you see the word *Bank*?'

The watchman reappeared with a superior. A moment later, the driver came back to the car.

'How much do you need? Give me the cheques, please.'

We said nothing for five long seconds, looking at each other past the sacks on our knees. A fuel tanker passed the car, blowing diesel through the open window. It was the only other vehicle in sight: the town was shutting down. So I pulled my shirt out of my trousers and groped for two traveller's cheques, and the man behind the grille disappeared with them.

'We're off our heads,' muttered Georgia.

'Is it the Tyebad bus, to the Afghan border?' said the blue-eyed man expectantly.

'It goes at four,' said Angela, 'There's not another till Monday.'

'Perhaps you would like to stay in Meshed? Well, no. But here we are…'

It was our money, with a smile and the hint of a bow.

'Now you want your bus tickets.'

He drove on. We had given themselves up to him. We said nothing until he stopped by a row of shops which were all closed, with steel shutters padlocked to heavy rings in the pavement. There were no customers or passers-by. Angela looked, and quivered.

'We're too late.'

'This is my office. You rest here, please, while we obtain your tickets.'

In Georgia's head, every rape alarm rang, every tocsin – but we had surrendered. We got out of the car, tugging weakly at the rucksacks whose aluminium frames jammed in the door. Stuck inside, Georgia tried to push. From nowhere, from some shadow, a Persian youth scuttled to the kerb and laid hands on the bags, saying 'Yes, yes!' as he slipped them out deftly.

Georgia began to say, 'Leave that,' but had not the strength.

'Mahmoud will take two,' said the driver, lifting the third bag himself.

There was a small office at the top of cement stairs, straight off the street. Benches upholstered in red vinyl lined the walls, and he switched on a standard fan which breathed left and right. There were grilles over the windows, with diamonds and peacocks in steel rod. The shutters were closed against the heat and the weekend.

'Take your rest now. There is a shower, if you wish. Please, give your bus money to Mahmoud.'

I didn't think twice, but Georgia snapped:

'For God's sake! You have to go with him.'

'Well…'

I dithered. The blue eyes looked at Georgia, whose wispy hair drifted across her face in the fan's breath.

'It is better if you let Mahmoud go alone,' said our rescuer. 'It may not be easy to find tickets, especially if they see foreigners. They may put the price up too high. But please, discuss this. I am going out for some minutes. I will be back shortly.'

He moved noiselessly out of the room. Young Mahmoud waited, patient, in a grey skullcap.

Angela fled straight to the bathroom, clutching a towel and a soap bag: there came a flatulent, liquid noise of disease. I pushed my hair off my forehead. Georgia perched on the red vinyl bench, her voice rising as the fan reinvigorated her.

'We have no idea, *no idea* who these people are, and that is all our money for the weekend.'

'We'll cash cheques in Afghanistan.'

'How do you know? There may not be any tickets. Whose office is this, do we know even that? We don't know the man's name and you're going to trust this brat with hundreds…'

'You can go if you like,' I said.

Astonished, she stared at me, and then glanced at the doorway. The man was there, watching her without expression. They looked straight at each other, her orange hair twisted in mistrust, his blue eyes steady. Then he turned away and descended. Georgia lay back on the red vinyl bench with her face to the ceiling and her eyes closed.

When the man returned, he was carrying a bag from which the scent of kebabed meat and chilli curled. Angela nibbled gingerly at a corner of bread. From his pocket, the man took a smaller, white paper bag and placed it on the bench.

'That is medicine for you, Miss. It will comfort you. You can certainly trust it.'

What was this talk of trust?

She held the little box, staring at the Farsi script as she chewed hot bread. Then she raised her head heavily and regarded the man with his grey hair and neat moustache, who sat now on the bench near her, his hands folded on his lap.

'Why are you doing all this?'

Dusty light from the shutters passed across his blue eyes.

'Ah, well,' he shrugged.

'But, why?'

'You know, I am missing my family.'

'Aren't they here?'

'They are in Turkey. I am Armenian; it is not easy to be Armenian in Iran. My family are at home, and I see them for three weeks each spring. We go out for many picnics when the wild cornflowers are best. But I am an architect and this is the office where I must work. I have no one to care for here, but for two hours today I can care for you. Do you mind?'

And there went through our young heads all sorts of reasons why we should mind, why these were suspect motives, as though the man had confessed to some form of deviancy.

We were asleep when Mahmoud returned with three bus tickets. The architect woke us and gave the tickets to Georgia.

'You, I think, should take care of these.'

He drove us to the Tyebad bus which waited in a crowded yard. Young men hammered wheel rims into massive tyres. Families clamoured and embraced. Here was life again! Of a sudden, I was once more a shrewd young traveller, sack on one shoulder, hair slicked. Angela put on sunglasses and began to smile. But the glare and the shouting, the glittering ragged ends of sawn steel and the mallets' ring hurt Georgia's head. A man seized her scarlet pack; she grabbed and cried sharply, 'No!' – then saw the grinning boys waiting on the roof.

She let go, insisting: 'You must tie it on.'

We shook the Armenian's hand, our thanks curiously reticent, for we were ashamed of ourselves. The Armenian regarded us with fondness. He took Georgia by her thin fingers and raised her onto the bus. She turned and held his hand a moment. He regarded her and nodded soberly, saying:

'Won't you promise to send me a card from Buckingham Palace?'

What I am left with now, all these decades later, is a prejudice in favour of Armenians – so much so that I react against it. I find that whenever I hear news of conflict between Armenia and Azerbaijan, it distresses me more than I can readily account for that one seldom hears the Azerbaijani point of view. I cannot bring myself to read books such as *Birds without Wings*, Louis de Bernière's account of the Armenian massacres in Turkey, because – having been so predisposed in favour of everything Armenian against anything Turkish or Iranian – I know I will resist with all my might, and doubt what I read almost on principle. There's the thanks you get for kindness.

The bus to Tyebad – a small town just short of the border – was packed with Afghans going home, filling the back seats with yards of cloth wrapped about every part of them, skull and chin, torso and feet all swathed in white wraps or in layer on layer of old overcoats. They clustered in the rear like springs tensed, all with a look of being on the verge of bursting out laughing. The usual helpful young Irani told us:

'They have no passports. They will bribe the police, or they will walk across the desert.'

Around us, the landscape was a brown waste apparently devoid of anything but shattered rock. Strangely, I could see sheep or goats of some sort in the distance, eating lichen apparently; there was nothing else. We had some two hundred kilometres to travel, starting at 4 p.m. Dusk fell. Perhaps half an hour before Tyebad, the Afghans began to clamour and the bus halted in the desert. They all tumbled out, gathered up their bundles and rushed away, making for low hills in the distance.

We crawled very late into Tyebad, a little cement town that in any decent Western movie would get thoroughly shot up. The Hotel Aria had an awfulness that was almost appealing. They gave us an upstairs room, stiflingly airless; Angela sank onto a cot and Georgia ministered, doling out medications. Otherwise she spent her time in flapping because she had mislaid her passport again, or in scribbling hurriedly in her diary.

Below in the courtyard there were bodies asleep in every shadow. Monstrous cockroaches stomped up and down the steep cement stairs outside, followed by a daft porter, the only person who took any interest in us, and who kept appearing at our door and gazing kindly at us slumped on our cots. He began to ask a long and incomprehensible question in Farsi. I got up and stood in front of him feeling helpless. He rested both his hands on my shoulders, leaned closer and placed a tender kiss on my forehead.

But it was the sickening Angela he was concerned for. He climbed back up bringing a plate of rice and cold goat stew. He handed this to Angela, smiling and nodding in his wisdom. Angela looked at the food, smiled bravely at him, regarded the food again and looked decidedly worse.

It was exactly the sort of establishment that Don Quixote would have mistaken for a nobleman's castle, with the ancient servant in the role of the duke's lovely daughter.

THREE

HEADLONG

These are no adventures of islands; these are only rencounters of
the road where little is to be got besides a broken head or the loss
of an ear. Therefore, have patience, and some adventure will offer
itself.

Don Quixote

On my return from India, I went back to college for the new term. At
dinner one evening I sat with an acquaintance chatting about our summer
adventures. He said that he too had been overland to the East; we
exchanged stories of the road.

'How did you travel?' I asked.

'It was fine,' he said. 'We went all the way by train.'

'How about Afghanistan?'

'Train the whole way,' he confirmed.

'You crossed Afghanistan by train? To Kabul?'

'Yes,' he insisted.

I could not think what to say; there are no trains across Afghanistan,
because there is no railway. Did he not know which country he was in?
Was he perhaps lying, having in fact passed the summer with his aunt at
Morecambe Bay? Perhaps to this day, among his family and friends some
regard him as a congenital fantasist, and some believe that he once crossed
that perilously romantic land by rail, and wish they had done so too –
though it makes me think of Turkish trains crossing the desert and being
shot to pieces by T.E.Lawrence and his friends.

Many people have dreamed of building railways in Afghanistan, usually
foreigners. A railway would have meant armies from Russia, British India
or Persia striking swiftly into the heart of the country, 'a knife in my vitals!'
as one Afghan ruler objected.

Such a railway was never built. There are in the entire country only a
few kilometres of line at the borders, the tail ends of links from
Turkmenistan and Uzbekistan. Latterly, with British troops occupying

Afghanistan for the fourth time since the 1830s, work supposedly got under way to bring the Iranian line from Meshed over the border to Afghan Herat. In theory, the railway will sweep south through Helmand Province, east to Kandahar, then north again to Kabul – the route that I travelled by bus – avoiding the mountain massif in the centre of the country.

Little has been constructed. Unless NATO does better at subjugating the countryside than the British in the 1840s, 1880s and 1919, or the Russians in the 1980s, an Afghan railway will remain as illusory as my Cambridge friend's journey in 1974.

Georg Simmel, in *Das Abenteuer,* wrote:

An adventure recalled takes on a dreamlike quality... The more adventurous an adventure... the more dreamlike it seems in recollection. It may move so far from the ego's centre... that we may think of it as experienced by another person.

And yet it will thereafter have a central importance in our lives; this was Simmel's idea of the adventure. It is as though there are two persons involved: oneself, and the adventure-self who one hopes will send back despatches from the periphery, and who may be lying or hallucinating. Perhaps my friend's fantasy train ride has real importance for him. When I look at photographs of myself on the road to the East (I have just two), it is as though the scruff who smiles back at me is an envoy from whom I still await news.

I don't know what the journey means now to my companions; I know only that Angela filled her London home with oriental crafts, while Georgia became an Asian anthropologist. Recalling 1974 today might embarrass them.

A minibus to the Iran-Afghan border, and a flurry of drug arrests. The Iranians were cracking down, and various unfortunates sitting in the police station were being told that they'd get four years. A story circulated among the waiting travellers that a motor-caravan had passed through yesterday, and had been discovered to be carrying many kilos of marijuana packed in its double skin.

Today, a battered old bus was parked in the Iran border-post compound; the passengers were young and French, on their way home. A girl with lank hair and faded cottons approached us:

'India is so hot, you walk in the street and you must drink so you see that he is selling cold drink and always it is one rupee for one drink, one more rupee for one more drink, it is expensive but of course India is beautiful and Nepal is so wonderful but now I am very tired, you have a cigarette?'

More joyous were a gaggle of Mombasa Kenyans, big boned men in white robes with smiles as ample as their suitcases. Their leader offered me a biscuit. Everything seemed to please him, even the Customs officer fingering his belongings in the open suitcase.

'We are called Islam Brothers and now we are going to a great school of Islam which is in Lahore and we are happy because we have waited many years to go. And will you come and stay too? Yes, it is very fine and you may stay with us. Here, I will give you the address...'

Georgia and I sat on the steps eating a melon between us and watching the Afghan lorries, which were like carousel horses on wheels; venerable Bedfords and Chevrolets were encrusted with tiny mirrors and intricate paintwork in rainbow colours, every surface subdivided into blue lozenges and purple scrolls. Out of this bulged freight that towered high above the sides, a dough of new goods rising out of its tin in the heat and barely constrained by grubby tarpaulins. Was it conceivable that Customs should actually search these? It would be half a day's work simply to untie the boxes. Drivers and officials drifted about the compound, clasping triplicates and regarding each other with apprehension, cunning or relish. The officials had nothing to interest them except some pretty Dutch girl in Tibetan garments whom they could delay an hour over a passport technicality.

Georgia pointed out a truck whose decoration included roundels of British redcoats marching with shouldered arms, a mocking echo of General Elphinstone's retreat from Kabul in 1842, in which virtually his entire column of 16,000 was slaughtered by the Pashtun.

We boarded an Afghan minibus in company with the Islam Brothers and a pleasant German couple called Hans and Anneliese. The minibus free-wheeled downhill to the Afghan border post, a small cement building on its own in the desert where a young rifleman leafed through the passports. He lingered over Anneliese's yellow vaccination booklet, turning and returning the pages.

'Wackseen!'

'Yes, please?'

'Wackseen! Wackseen!'

The soldier motioned to the driver to let her out. Anneliese protested.

'But I have vaccine, look, it is here.'

She pointed to the certificates – but something was wrong.

'No wackseen!'

The soldier, holding the booklet open in one hand, thumped it with his other fist: the German doctor had signed but had not stamped the cholera certificate. Two more soldiers carrying rifles came out of the guard post. They pulled open the minibus door.

'Wackseen! Wackseen! Wackseen!'

The Germans were led into the guard house under armed escort.

Angela murmured: 'Shit, she'll get hepatitis from the needle, poor kid.'

'But I think these soldiers are just,' replied Mohammed of the Islam Brothers. 'Many soldiers would be asking for money.'

The Germans reappeared, unescorted. Anneliese, in tears, nursed a bare arm. Hans nursed Anneliese.

We continued in silence.

The highway rolled through fawn rocks towards Herat, each village we passed like a squat mud fort outside which the goats and the camels mooched. Near several of these little redoubts were scattered encampments of nomads, their tattered hair tents spun out across the stony dust like limpets before the village.

Knots of riders clattered along the highway on ponies, their saddles smothered under swathes of cloth, and each carrying a rifle, WWII army surplus, not the long *jezails* that picked off Elphinstone's army in the Kabul gorges. Some of the tribesmen let their rifles dangle easily at their flank, while others bore theirs proud and upright like Mr Punch bearing his member before him to the stupefaction of young ladies.

Angela had been in Kabul in July a year before; she had been woken in the night by the sound of automatic rifle fire. In the early morning, fighter aircraft had skimmed across the city, and the hotel staff had rushed from room to room shouting that there had been a revolution and that all the generals had been shot. (In fact it had been a bloodless putsch, as King Zahir had been at an Italian health farm at the time). Angela and her companions went out to see what was afoot and, in amongst the crowds, one of her friends had his pouch (money, passport, tickets, cheques) stolen. But martial law had been declared, and the police were quite uninterested in his problems. He then caught hepatitis. Angela and the others eventually had to leave him in Kabul, and it took him weeks to get out.

Stories like this we told each other with grim relish, while checking our documents yet again.

Herat now was tricked out for the anniversary of the 'revolution', with black, red and green tricolours everywhere. Civic pride was on the up; since Robert Byron passed this way in 1934, they'd paved two thoroughfares and opened an airline office, and had planted an abundance of petunias. In the centre of town, in the middle of a dusty parterre was a civic pond, circular with blue cement walls. Here the republican flags were thickest and here on the water was a revolutionary paddleboat. It had a wooden frame about twelve feet long, covered with a heavy black fabric and rising to an awkwardly curved prow where was propped a large portrait photograph of the usurper Daud. To symbolise progress, the boat was driven by a splendid arrangement of three paddle-wheels, big wooden contraptions powered by the captain's arm, with one at the prow to steer. A few turns of this to left or right altered the course.

Even a short voyage was an exercise in stamina and coordination for the Pashtun boatman who would take three or four children at a time for a spin around the pond while other citizens leapt into the water fully clothed, though with their turbans carefully laid aside.

Tribesmen rode by, rifle at the hip, looking contemptuous of the mere notion of travel by water.

In Hotel Mohmand, Hans and Anneliese snuggled up in their sleeping bags on our balcony. At last I felt that we were getting somewhere – and when today I look at the nostalgia websites, I find that others shared the feeling that Iran did not quite count: the East began at Afghanistan.

There were swap-shops in Herat, cluttered with junk: redundant boots, defunct cameras, hot jeans traded for light soft cottons. This was where the travellers began to shed their skins, and certain inhibitions also. When I look now at photographs of myself in an Afghan shirt, it is with dismay. Never again have I looked anything like that. My hair is lank and long, parted to one side and draped down to my shoulders. I am unshaven in a fluffy, unprepossessing way, my clothing is grey and rudimentary – an appalling spectacle, whether standing alongside the pert flowery figure of Georgia, or any Pashtun tribesman, or any modern young Afghan functionary in a crisp cotton uniform. All I can say in self-defence is that I seem very cheerful, and that many other travellers looked much the same.

What did young Afghans think of us? Did we really represent an aspiration? In a swap-shop I dumped a jersey which I replaced with Herat shirts of cool but simple cut: no collar, but with buttons at the neck. Georgia exchanged a bundle of English goods for one small water bottle and then felt swindled, although the large water bottle she had traded in leaked, as someone else would discover later. Angela lumbered herself with a large Japanese lacquered parasol, and a capacious double saddlebag made of richly worked wool. Angela's own considerable bulk, the embroidered saddlebags, her vast blue rucksack and the Japanese parasol made an extraordinary ensemble whenever she sallied out to an overcrowded bus or train. She was in her element now, surrounded by admirers and shopkeepers some of whom truly seemed to recognise her from the year before. In every shop Georgia and I would be served bitter black tea but Angela would wangle a free Coke. Georgia looked good in her new clothes, a cool little suit of loose cotton which showed up her small, boyish body. It was decided that she was to marry Gellir, a young shoemaker. I meanwhile had fallen for Gellir's twelve-year-old brother John, whose eyes purred at me in soft mischief. Gellir agreed that if Georgia would marry him he would make her a pair of sandals very cheap. John made me a shirt very cheap because I promised to send all my friends to his shop. He had my photograph and I had his. His hair was short and soft, like the fur of a black cat; his eyebrows were the same. In the family shop was a clutter of wooden benches, leather and bicycles, and a large mirror round the frame of which were stuck dozens of passport photographs, their gallery of 'all our friends from your country.'

A history of Herat: the original fort was built by Alexander the Great. In the 7th century it was first captured by Muslims. In 1040 the town was destroyed by the Seljuk Turks. In 1221 Herat was captured by the Mongols, with the death of 12,000 defenders. Soon afterwards, local tribes rebelled and Genghis Khan arrived with 80,000 men to lay siege to the town which held out for six months, by which time there were reputedly only forty people left within the walls. In 1381 Herat was razed by Tamerlane. In 1507, it was besieged and captured by the Uzbeks, and in 1749 was taken by the Pashtuns… and so on. (The Taleban, and heavy bombing by the Russians, the mujahedin resistance, Al Qaeda and NATO were all still to come.)

The facts were stated dryly in a little leaflet, in English, available free of charge in the bank. I'd gone in to change some traveller's cheques. I handed over my passport which was very old, first issued when I was eleven. The cashier looked at the cheques that I had just signed, and again at the passport.

'Sir, the signature on the cheque is not the same as the signature in the passport.'

It was quite true; in the passport was the scratchy signature of an eleven-year-old. No one had remarked this before.

'Does it matter?' I asked.

'Oh yes, sir. I cannot cash your cheque if they are not the same.'

'But look, this is my signature when I was very young. Look, there is a photograph of me when I was eleven. But you see, underneath is a photo of me as I am now, where it says *Wife*.'

'Yes sir, I can see that it is a photograph of you. Perhaps you can put your new signature here, where it says: *Signature of wife*?'

'A good idea.'

I signed again, in the space marked *wife*.

'That is good, sir. Now the signatures are the same and we know you are the same person, and I shall give you your money.'

I went out into the streets, past shops selling rugs made up of twenty-five fox pelts. Something that Tamerlane would not have seen in 1381 were the piles of South American potatoes in the marketplace. On her previous visit, said Angela, there had been no cars in Herat. Buses and

trucks, but no cars. There was a handful now: Fiats, Ambassadors from India, a few Volkswagens. In 1934 Robert Byron observed the installation of a policeman on a bandbox at Herat's central crossroads, who whistled furiously at any tonga that came within earshot. But he must have got bored, and had left.Here were gentlemen with piercing black eyes smoking and scrutinising me from the foot of mud walls; over there was a woman shrouded in black sitting quite still in the middle of a lane. Here was a baker; the oven was a hole in the ground, a pit with a fire burning in the bottom. The flat ovals of dough had to be lowered down through the hole and slapped onto the overhanging wall. One man had the job of leaning into the hole to slap them on and peel them off; he seemed addled by the heat, and twitched continually. The men – in turban, waistcoat or tailored jacket – sat cross-legged by the pit regarding me with faintly ironic smiles. Behind these, another man weighed something on a brass balance held in mid-air, and children skulked under the dark vaults behind.

I lost myself in back lanes where holes in the mud-brick walls of houses let the sewage and rats out into a deep gutter. A very few people, walking silently: black draped women, white draped men, shapes and shadows passing across walls, surfaces articulated only by patches of mud rendering and occasional wooden poles jutting out at an angle – or, even rarer, by the dark square of a window, high up. From time to time there was a door of antediluvian white boards. As I passed one, it opened and a very beautiful small girl in a faded blue smock emerged and studied me with great interest. She saw the camera in my hand and reached out a finger to touch the lens – but at that moment a veiled figure reached through the opening, seized her and tweaked her back inside, slamming the door in my face. In a small square, where men sat on low ledges along the walls of houses, another crone closed in on me, laughing, tugging at the camera, pointing at herself, shrieking with laughter again, posing, thrusting her chin out at me, pointing once more at the camera and at her own face, striking as majestic an attitude as she could, hooting all the while. But the turbaned men watching this did not approve at all; they stepped forward with angry waves and imprecations and shooed me away. I began to feel lost, even

threatened. Over these lanes, the citadel glowered; this was the town almost as Tamerlane would have seen it, if he bothered to look before he razed it all – the world that the Taleban fight to preserve.

The wind was rising in Herat; the dust was hard on the eyes. I retreated to a teashop where a customer was playing an Afghan lute – a *rubab* – the music quick and cheerful. This was what I wanted.

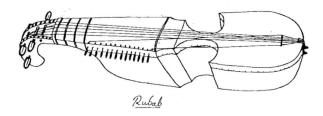

Rubab

Another man was drumming casually; a second drum was on the bench beside me, and I began a pattering at which they smiled and nodded, at once politely encouraging and embarrassed.

Outside, the tribesmen galloped about the town pulling their scarves across their faces. Or waited at the roadside for a bus.

At 5 a.m. someone kicked open the door of our hotel room and screamed that it was late, that the Qaderi Bus Company would not delay. I would much rather have gone by train.

It took eighteen hours to reach Kabul, driving in a great saggy southerly loop to Kandahar and then north-east again to the capital, always with treeless beige mountains to our left. The country looked blasted with dryness – indeed, there had been three years of drought in which 70,000 or more people had died of starvation. By 1974, the Russians, the Americans and the Chinese were all supplying food aid, although none of this had been apparent in Herat. Every village that we passed through was decked out for the joyful anniversary of the Republic: pink crêpe archways outside tiny hamlets, tricolours on every building. Over the bus radio they played eulogies followed by panegyrics followed by martial tunes, hour after hour.

In the stony wilderness of southern Afghanistan, there were tiny settlements near the roadside, perhaps only a single mud house. Here was one thatched with brushwood, and small donkeys looking famished and sorrowful as ever. Who are these two men? One appears to be a proprietor, a trader (trading what, out here?) who is weighing something in a balance. The balance is remarkable in itself: not the neat brass scales of Herat bazaar. This is a tree-trunk (but there are no trees) set not quite vertically in the ground. From its knobbly top hangs a length of wire and from the lower end of that dangles a cross-beam, another bough of rare wood. Below this cross piece hang two home-made wire cradles. Some deal or assay is being done. The proprietor, in his turban, his loose whites and brown waistcoat, seems to have the whip hand – the other (who has maybe brought something to sell) looks younger and browbeaten. It is not a scene of roaring commerce. In the background, some thirty paces away, is another tree trunk, this one perhaps over a well.

All this seems fairly clear in the photograph, but my diary says: 'At one stop there was a small thatched house with a well, the occupant pulling up water for his two donkeys with a simple counterbalanced dipper.' Which should I now trust: the observation noted down within a few hours, or my reading of the picture made forty years later?

Elsewhere was a cemetery by the road, an un-boundaried tract of stones some of which stood upright. Nearby, a man – watchman? goaterd? beggar? – sat under a shelter of matting like a weal in the ground. Further off were the tents of nomads, poor patched things clinging to a devastated landscape. In the background, always mountains.

A WEAL IN THE
GROUND, A GOATHERD
SITTING UNDER IT.

It was very hot in the bus; the plastic seats grew stickier, the water in our bottles more metallic and tepid by the minute. Received wisdom held that it was unwise to travel to the East with someone of the opposite sex merely as friends – or as lovers – as this would offer no protection against the lasciviousness of the natives who would understand this arrangement as symptomatic of a moral laxity which they were thereby encouraged to take advantage of. So we had been taking it in turns to declare that Georgia was my wife and Angela her sister, or vice versa. Angela's fair hair had a reddish tinge to it which helped, for Georgia's was positively orange. But we sometimes forgot whose turn it was. The bus seated four abreast; Georgia – today's sister-in-law – found herself sitting next to a colonel of the Afghan Army. He was quite a handsome man in his soft way, with a smooth, slightly weak face that belonged in a 1950s Graham Greene story. He was fond of showing everyone a wallet of snaps of his wife and children. When I proposed to take a photograph of Georgia and him, the colonel drew himself upright in his seat, put on his steeply peaked cap and narrowed his eyes at the lens.

But later, Georgia leaned across to me in the darkening bus and said with exaggerated slowness that there was a hand creeping under her thigh. We stood and changed over seats. Attempts to glare at the colonel for this affront to my sister-in-law failed; he mopped his brow and looked ahead. An hour later, I detected a hand creeping under my thigh. I tucked it firmly back in its owner's crotch. We did not look at each other.

Looking now at my several poor grey photos of Georgia and the colonel, taken on that bus, I am struck with the poignancy. Georgia, nearest the camera, has a bandana about her head, and she looks at the lens with an expression of quite childish, nose-in-the-air, wide-eyed defiance, as though I've demanded to know what she thinks she is doing there. Behind her, the colonel in his cap holds onto the seat in front and does his best to look shrewd. In another picture, he gazes straight at me. It is not a very martial face, and I cannot imagine him among the rocks in the Kabul gorges in 1842, ambushing General Elphinstone. As he peers back at the camera, I now wonder what role he had played in the previous year's revolution; whether he would survive the coming coup of 1978 in which the Army overthrew and executed President Daud whose advent we were now all celebrating; whether he fought with the Russians against themujahedin, or took off his uniform to lead his countrymen against yet another bunch of invaders; whether he was taken out and shot by his own regiment, died in a roadside blast, or is today in retirement and playing with his grandchildren? If he is still alive, he'll be in his eighties now at least; I wonder what he thinks and fears, as the Taleban and Afghan government fight over just the territory through which our bus was now

70

travelling, where not long ago British troops hardly dared move for fear of explosives in the roadside, but called for helicopters. And there behind the bus to the north of the road is the central massif of Afghanistan, where no one in his right mind ever goes without permission.

Every few hours, the bus would stop and let us off for a few minutes; usually there was little more than a ditch to get off for, although a chance to splash a handful of water over our freely sweating faces was welcome. That is Hans in the photo scooping up water, and Anneliese dressed in black nearer the bus.

At one halt there were three tiny huts in the desert, and in the shade of one stood a fine, dignified figure. To his left, a pile of musk melons. To his right, a pile of water melons. On top of the latter, a crate of Coke. Outside Kandahar there were food and drink stalls, a recognised victualling point for all buses. The colonel tucked into chicken stew and Coke. Two Pakistani brothers swaggered up and down in identical T-shirts declaring both men to be *USA AMERICAN*, together with identical and brand new white baseball caps and identical brand new black attaché cases, from which they were inseparable.

A miserable introduction to Kabul. At 11 p.m. the Qaderi Company put us down in a dark bus park, the colonel vanished in a staff car, and the hotel touts pounced. The representative of Friends Hotel, particularly eager, offered us a free taxi and so we went with him. The hotel – a detached cement villa with broad stairways and wide windows – looked as though in better days it might have housed the British Council. We slumped onto our beds. No sooner had I closed my eyes than Angela was hitting me.

'I don't like to see bedbugs walking across my friends.'

We kicked the mattresses out onto the landing and slept on the rush stringing of the charpoys.

In the morning I went down to pay the fat hotelier who sat in a little booth like a Punch-and-Judy theatre in the garden. This was his office. I handed over a large note and waited for the change, hoping to avoid an argument about bed bugs.

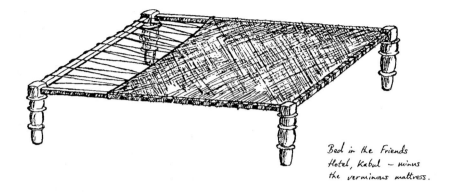

Bed in the Friends Hotel, Kabul — minus the verminous mattress.

'You come last night in my car?'
'Yes, from the Herat bus.'
'You go today?'
'That's right.'
'Then this pay for car.'
'You said it was free.'
'No free for one night.'
'You said it was free. Give me that back!'
'No free.'
'I shall call the police!'
(Unconcerned shrug.)
'Give me that...'

I attempted to grab the large note back, at which the fat hotelier took up a plastic ruler and started smacking my hand. His staff were closing in. I retreated to the bedroom in chagrin and told my story. There was a young Irishman sharing with us, on his way to Australia; I asked him not to pay for his bed.

'OK,' he said, 'but I don't have any small notes I can give you. I've got these boots that I don't want. You could sell them...'

How much more soundly Don Quixote would have dealt with the fat hotelier. We marched out in a phalanx, and removed ourselves to the pleasant and peaceful Green Hotel near the centre of town. There appeared to be only three rooms: one for the three of us, one empty, and one for a girl from New Zealand recovering from hepatitis.

Almost next door was Sigi's, a famous name, a major milestone on the road to the East. It was known for the constant supply of free green tea simmering in a large brown kettle on an electric ring under the arcades, and its unrivalled status as a rendezvous. Here sat the travellers, resident and non-resident, dining on cheese omelettes and swallowing endless green tea, or padding softly in flip-flops to the shower, towel on arm. They were changing, becoming noticeably quieter, more withdrawn, perhaps counting themselves lucky to have got so far. This passed for calm.

Music was a comfort. Sigi's proprietor was a German who sat in state playing scratchy vinyl LPs of Beethoven, which made his establishment feel safer. Although no one possessed a Walkman, some travellers had bulky tape players with them, and cassettes of Led Zeppelin. They greeted each other in a murmur:

'Hey, you here now? Listen, really, you want to come down the place I'm at. There's three Swedish guys with their whole stereo and some really amazing folk music...'

That wasn't what I had come for – but I had little idea how to find anything more local. Until I had some luck: I sat on a bench in a shop in the bazaar watching a man make a *rubab,* an Afghan lute. He was a nice man, pleased to have a visitor watch him shape the *rubab* with a rasp. Bald and shy, he obviously wanted to play for me, and tried, but his left hand was so wounded with cuts and calluses that he could not finger properly and gave up the attempt, holding out his hand to show me, and smiling apologetically.

Today, I have a Moroccan lute hanging on my wall, a Nepalese bowed lute in the attic, a sitar leaning in the corner, a Javanese spike-lute wired to the ceiling, and an eight-course English lute called a Woodlark in a black case, together with two dozen other instruments from half a dozen countries, almost all of them humble things made in homes and backstreets. But this I think was the first I watched being made.

We ate one night in a restaurant which had a board outside advertising 'real Afghan music with your dinner.' We sat on cushions in the dark carpeted room off which we ate *ashak* – a ravioli made with mint, spinach and yoghurt, and excellent. But the music was poor and unskilled.

The heat did not let up, and by now both Angela and Georgia were sick, one with the runs, one with a fever. Georgia was covered in bites, especially her lower legs, some small and weeping, some broad red weals that stood out from her rapidly reddening skin. No hepatitis yet. We were stuck idle for a day as everything closed for the speechifying and sports in honour of the Revolution, and there was little for foreigners to do but mooch about and avoid the sun. If I'd been an English gentleman on the Grand Tour in Rome *c*.1760, I'd have used the time to commission a portrait from Pompeo Batoni. In Kabul I bought shawls in the old bazaar, creamy coloured and embroidered at each end. Looking back, I am surprised at how much we acquired so early in the journey, burdening ourselves; I would travel so much lighter now. Yet I wish I could remember where those shawls got to.

In Sigi's and the Green Hotel there was just one guest who was neither Afghan nor a westerner. Panya was a young Indian. He declared that he had seen all of India, had dropped university sciences and, provoked by the freedom of Western youth, had determined to travel to Europe. It had taken him five months to smuggle enough money out of India. Now almost penniless, he was heading for Switzerland, living on tea and bread. I wondered if he still thanked us for unsettling him so. As I write this, the French government is rounding up penniless aliens from squalid camps in the woods outside Calais, Asian migrants all waiting for a chance to jump lorries crossing to Dover. Many are reported to be Afghans.

We planned to reach Nepal by the end of the month, just ten days away; we now had tickets for a bus over the Khyber Pass. We longed for time to be still, to be able to absorb more, but always we hurtled forward, needing to be further on and perhaps enjoying the scuttling for its own sake. In my diary I wrote that, 'It's like rushing headlong into a field of unidentified herbs hoping to be far in before you trip and fall, crushing your face into them.'

As the girls recovered, they began hankering: for cereals with milk, for chicken sandwiches, and for affection. A letter had reached the *poste restante* from Angela's father, and she fingered it and re-read it whenever she thought we were not looking. We had been away from home just two weeks.

In the bazaar, Georgia found something for me. She presented this to me with her usual diffident shrug: 'I thought, this would be just the sort of thing Jo likes'.

It was a most peculiar knife. When closed it looked like some sort of exotic measuring instrument: a set of tappet gauges for an Afghan lorry, perhaps, in a case of cunningly hinged brass.

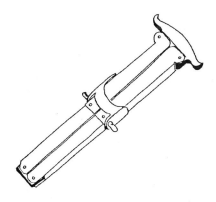

Lift the catch, pull the sides of the case outwards, and the hingeing movement thrust the blade forward.

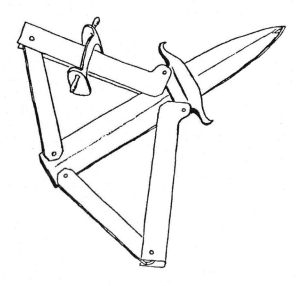

The case then closed behind it, forming the handle. There was something remarkably phallic in its thrust forward, the brass thighs closing and tightening behind the blade thrust.

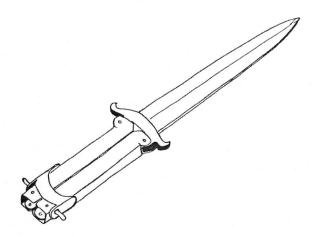

The interior of the bus on the Peshawar run was clad with a green marble laminate. Heavy chains were stowed under the back seat, and were thrown noisily to and fro by the potholes; it was like riding inside a giant Byzantine tambourine. It was half-full, cool and fast – very fast: a gypsy's ass with quicksilver in its ear, as Sancho Panza had recently remarked of Rozinante. It whipped up the dust along valley roads by powdery pale blue rivers. Here, in 1842, Elphinstone's troops had staggered through the dreadful winter being picked off by the *jezail* muskets, whose flintlocks were taken off British muskets but whose range was far longer, so that the British could not strike back. Five years after we passed through, this territory was devastated by the Russians.

I have found a Russian army veterans' website of photographs from their 1979-89 Afghan war; they look like very distant memories. Some are tourist views of mosques and roundabouts in Kandahar, Herat and Kabul; one shows a monument in Kabul that commemorates the Afghan defeat of the British at Maimand in July 1880. The colour is crude and primitive, with an almost hand-tinted look. Others are black-and-white snaps of Russian soldiers, gathered in matey huddles like a football team, or surveying crashed vehicles, or sitting around coffee tables. In one, captioned 'Cavalry', a large Russian sits astride a little mule saddled only with sacking, the tall soldier's legs trailing to the ground, his trousers turned up to the knee and his AK47 slung across his chest. The young soldiers seem bashed about by sun, stones, *jezails* and their own Kalashnikovs in tribal hands. The young men look unloved and uncared for, with the sad bonhomie of cannon-fodder. Some lie in field hospitals; one has both legs gruesomely mangled from a landmine explosion. That particular young man may be making his painful way about Russia to this day. Many of the black-and-white prints are badly battered; they look to have been salvaged from the private albums of the troops, or found in a shoebox also containing grandfather's snaps of the Stalingrad campaign.

It all seems to come from a very distant time, and it is strange to think that these events and photos date from well after our journey. Simmel says of the adventure, that one of its defining characteristics is that its temporal bounds are clear. There is a clear-cut beginning and end. Those Russians may now look back on their time in Afghanistan as a Simmel-esque bad dream, a misadventure. Curiously, in his consideration of types of adventure, Simmel does not mention war.

In July 1974, we rattled away to Pakistan, up the Khyber Pass in our green marbled bus, at once thankful for and alarmed by its speed. There were the old forts, as massive and brutish as the day they were built, awe-inspiring if you imagined a musket at every loophole, but pathetic if you looked at the little redoubts on the surrounding hills, all in visual contact with the mother fort but what good would that do you when the middle ground was swarming with tribesmen, and you were out of range of a British Brown Bess but in range of the *jezails*?

I could have used Georgia's folding knife to stab the station master in Peshawar. I was petitioning for student concessionary rates, and he wanted only a long conversation about the operation of railways in our two countries. I sat among the magnificent wooden fittings of his office, sweating freely and trying to hide my urge to thump the table and bawl at him... but at last he sighed and signed the form. The sweat had soaked the leather thong of the pouch about my neck; I had a dark brown stripe diagonally down the back of my shirt.

But we were hurtling along now, on an overnight train from Peshawar to Lahore. In the hours of darkness, there was a change: we fell asleep in a dry tawny country and awoke amidst red soils, saturated greens, saturated everything, thick humid heat. We lingered only to check the *poste restante* and to eat in an air conditioned Chinese restaurant, the meal strained, both girls grumpy and snappish; nothing pleased them. We were filthy, smelly, shitty, exhausted and ridiculously cold. This was as far as Angela had managed the previous year, and she was wondering, again, if she would make it to India.

Still we must hurry. The border closed early and we were suddenly panicking for transport. Then a huddle of men saw us:

'Taxi to India?'

We bundled in, sacks on our laps, together with a silent gentleman in civilian clothes who nursed on his lap a revolver in a leather holster. We passed graffiti on the walls of Lahore demanding that we *Crush India*. The driver, hurrying, knocked a man off his bicycle and didn't look back. There was little time left, but the Pakistani officials spoke in sentences of painful slowness, as though rather hurt by our departure but believing that it must be some sad duty that drew us to the East, that we must be touched by their poignant, lingering farewell.

Angela began to weep. At this, they waved us on down the refulgent avenue that led out of Pakistan, lush to the point of alcoholic: green dripped from top-heavy trees, red and green parrots clustered in the branches. We staggered eastward under our absurd great rucksacks like marathon runners about to collapse only yards from the line – until, beyond a painted line on the road, a single soldier emerged from a wooden sentry box, beamed at us and said:

'But this is India.'

FOUR

THIN AIR

Dr Munshi declared, 'You must fly.'

'We had thought of going by bus.'

'Bus? At this time of year? And you want to be in Kathmandu by the end of the month? My dear boy, the lowland roads will be flooded and the mountain roads blocked by a dozen landslides.'

I looked crestfallen. Dr Munshi regarded me sternly.

'You don't like what I am saying, do you? It is not the image, perhaps? But you must fly; you have no choice. You must swallow your pride.'

Dr Munshi, our Delhi contact, was surely right – though it hurt to be told.

We had rushed headlong across Asia to make our rendezvous. We had missed sights, skipped cultures, scurried on to reach Nepal in time. We had passed through cities without sleeping, ignored entire regions in our urge to keep moving. We flew up to Kathmandu at great expense and then spent a long day in a cramped minibus winding through drenched Himalayan valleys, lurching over landslips and twisting along riversides hour on hour, all to be here in time to stay with Eric – Eric the medical student, Eric at the Shining Hospital. We got out in a dark street late at night and walked two miles in pitch black and pouring rain, lugging our rucksacks. And came at last to the tin-roofed mission hospital to find Eric.

Eric had left the day before. He had left no message. To hell with Eric.

Angela sat on the steps of the doctor's house, and stared blankly out into the rain. Georgia sat beside her, and announced quietly that she wasn't moving. This did not leave the resident British doctor and his wife with a great deal of choice.

They had been there fourteen years. They gave us a shower, a dry towel each, and beds with mosquito nets. They gave us coffee, fried eggs and home-made bread with thick buffalo cream in lieu of butter. In the morning, there was brown porridge and more coffee. As soon as our clothes were dry, we moved away, painfully aware of our frivolous youth.

We made for the lakeside, hoping that we had at least halted our headlong rush.

Pokhara is now the capital of the Himalayan trekking industry, with international chain hotels, a new hospital, and technical colleges. In 1974 it was a grubby village in the Himalaya. By the lake – now lined with luxury guest houses – there were then just a few 'lodges' for the likes of us, clusters of small mud buildings, thatched and fenced and given a name: Phewa Lodge, Lake Lodge, Annapurna Lodging. In each there would be one or two huts divided into rooms for the guests, also one for the family, and another for the kitchen with a porch and a few tables and chairs surrounded by succulents and fire lilies.

At night it poured with rain; the air sang with mosquitoes, and when one stepped out for a pee the mud in the yard popped with frogs. Sometimes a firefly passing low would light up the eyes of the frogs, blinking and full of mystique, like little Fu Manchus in the mud. Often it was pitch dark. We had an oil lamp in our room, but the family in their single small hut seemed to have no light at all, not even to cook by.

It was delightful. It was neat and the red mud was swept clean, and if the latrine was out in the yard, well, so it was at my house in Cambridge. From the cheerful family to the trim little huts, the clean sheets and the red blankets on the beds, the racket of frogs and rain and the glow of the lamp, the effect was entirely charming. It was almost deserted; the Kathmandu buses had gone on strike and, though there was an airstrip, flights were prohibitively costly. So we were more or less trapped and perfectly happy about it. Pokhara was less happy to have its tourist trade cut off. The lodge family were relieved to have anyone there at all, and even more thrilled when an Australian couple arrived on a big BMW motorbike.

We calmed down in the thin, damp air.

Above the village, Annapurna was in cloud. After the evening storm, the rain had eased to a gentle liquid caress, while the streams and ditches poured a thin muddy effluent into the lake from all sides, in such volumes that I imagined the waters must rise and fill the entire valley until we all floated higher up. The lake – Phewa Tal – had no firm boundaries, only flooded fields being stirred up by oxen dragging ploughs.

I have a single decaying box of colour slides taken at Pokhara in 1974.

At the time I was the proud owner of a Soviet-made projector called an 'Educator'. It was very small and primitive; it had no fan, just a cast metal case with fins, and it made the slides so hot that they popped and twisted in front of the lamp. To my delight I find that my father-in-law has the same model, bought in Aden in 1955, which he lends to me – so I can glimpse the colours of Pokhara again, on Fuji transparencies that emphasise the green tones.

Peering at these now, projected on a patch of white wall in Scotland, at first glance it all looks very sweet. Phewa Tal is placid and ringed by steep hills, punctuated by an island temple, and with a scattering of dugout canoes. On the foreshore there are no modern buildings, only water-buffalo ploughing the paddy fields, steered by men under umbrellas. I see the neat bamboo fences and the walls with pretty ferns growing out of them; I see the children grinning from under brollies, surrounded by refulgent growth with little red tropeolums sparking amongst the green. Within the compounds, the red mud houses are often two-storey and thatched in an attractive stepped fashion with a row of small openings under the eaves, the window embrasures neatly trimmed in black paint.

But the thatch is sodden and grey with rot, and draped with bits of cotton and sacking, clothing and clouts. The compounds are littered with broken chairs and baskets, the ground itself green with algae. Ragged barefoot ragged children play, or sit on the walls holding brollies over their heads. In one slide, a father stands with his daughter, and they look to be damp and rotting also; he is probably thirty but appears fifty, while the little girl he clasps has thin, straggly lank hair; she looks malnourished and feverish. I can almost smell the tuberculosis in these pictures. There is water everywhere, dripping from the eaves, darkening the children's rags, swilling down the lanes, swelling innumerable streams which are crumbly, stony jumbles, quite unlike the hard granite or peat cleanliness of torrents in Scotland. In Nepal even the rain felt muddy. There's a slide of Georgia looking cheerful enough, smiling in her creamy flowered dress on a rock by a stream, her red hair plastered down by rain.

Was I shocked by the decay and self-evident disease at the time? I didn't record it. Perhaps I'm viewing the slides and the decay through the eyes of a tropical diseases nurse – a training I took more than a decade later.

I remember plenty of obstacles. Slippery green paths wound along the water margin, luring me into seas of mud across which I must flounder to find my way onward. In the lanes, I'd be nudged towards the ditch by a strolling buffalo or a small boy on an unstable bicycle pursued by his running sister, both squealing. I learned to dodge overhanging banana palms that poured out gouts of water when the breeze moved them. But I don't recall what I felt for the people – unless it is in the context of their homes. Everywhere in Nepal, I was photographing and thinking about people's homes.

Even the compound walls were most curious, a double frame of bamboo with stones packed between; the stone acquired a thick layer of moss, so it seemed that a solid bank had sprouted dozens of dead bamboos and succulents too, tall and spiny. Children popped up over the wall and shouted to terrify me – then giggled and wanted pictures taken. Their parents would be working in the rice fields by the lake, the men in drab but the women vivid, given to shocking pink scarves amongst the milk chocolate mud and the emerald vegetation.

Not far from our lodge, the houses thinned out and I could walk for twenty minutes without meeting anyone. I found a small building with a bench outside where I sat down. It was a tea shop, with half a dozen men on small stools in the gloom. There was tea and slabs of grey bread served by a beautiful nubile girl, and there was Jagath the *rentier*.

He had once been in a Gurkha regiment. These days he farmed and rented out a few cottages; he had some Germans in residence, painting. I said maybe I'd come back for a while and write, so he wrote his name across a page of *Don Quixote,* and suggested that I marry the pretty girl. She poured me another cup of tea and made herself scarce.

We exchanged compliments. He said:

'You are a clever Englishman. I wish to come to England to meet your Queen who is the daughter of my leader in battle.'

I drifted away, with a new friend and home and my married life sorted, quite content.

When we reached Pokhara, there seemed to be a change in all of us, a product of the lake, Phewa Tal. Angela pottered about smiling and adopting Nepalese children, and writing long letters home filled with drawings of village urchins. Georgia was sunburned and besotted with the lake, and bestowed significance upon every action:

'I only like swimming in solitude – it's sacred.'

or,

'Walking without shoes restores you to an awareness of the earth.'

We took an unstable dugout canoe over the placid lake, paddling slowly to a small inlet on the far shore where a stream came down to the shore. Georgia suddenly decided that this was the moment to abandon prurience and launched herself naked into the water. Angela sat on a rock in the stream toying with pebbles between her toes and slowly began to smile. It started to rain softly from hardly perceptible clouds, and the far end of the lake dissolved into a mist. A good swimmer, Georgia chugged out into the open on her back, glinting like unpolished silver in the milky sunlight. She turned, and splashed ashore just as three Nepalese men walked into view around a spur. Cervantes describes accurately what happened next:

> They approached so softly that she did not perceive them and, as she was paddling in the clear water, they had time to observe that her legs were white as alabaster. Our observers were amazed at this discovery. At the noise they made, the pretty creature started, and peeping through her hair, which she hastily removed from before her eyes with both her hands, she no sooner saw three men coming towards her, but in a mighty fright she snatched up a little bundle that lay by her and fled as fast as she could, without so much as staying to put on her shoes, or do up her hair. But alas! scarce had she gone six steps, when her tender feet not being able to endure the rough encounter of the stones, the poor affrighted fair fell on the hard ground.
>
> *Don Quixote*

I passed her a towel. We paddled home ever more slowly, shy of disturbing the surface of the water, not speaking.

But the tranquillity did not last more than a few days; now we had time, each of us was wondering what we were doing here. Why had we struggled all this way? What did we want from the East? Such self-questioning must have been common for young travellers: the effort of the journey had been its own *raison d'être* – but now what? Surrounded by so much beauty, we grew tense once more. Georgia became unsettled again, at one moment murmuring darkly that I was insensitive to the mountain calm, the next moment pulling out the map to ponder where she wanted to go next. Angela, still unwell, protested that she wanted nothing but peace and children to play with. But she was moping, disturbed by Georgia's restlessness, pining for her man in London, unable to reconcile her homesickness with the realisation of her dream of India and Nepal. She would cry silently because there had been no letters for her at any *poste restante* anywhere.

'I suppose I'm discovering myself, though,' she'd whimper, cheering up after a long talk and something to eat.

There was, in the lodge next door, a Canadian girl staying. She had been travelling in Asia for eighteen months. Each morning, her Nepalese boyfriend would arrive with a bicycle for her and a bicycle for himself. She was rather lovely, with long wavy hair and a fresh, open face. Her boyfriend treated her with elaborate courtesy and tenderness. She seemed calm and content; she made us feel by comparison that we were in some sort of a state most of the time, and we each harboured a desire to achieve something like her calm. But then she revealed that she was beginning to grow weary, and was wanting to go home.

Five hundred yards along the shore, a Nepalese crown prince was also staying, with a platoon of Gurkhas and bathing restricted in that part of Phewa Tal; his tranquillity depended upon bodyguards. I suspected him of being grossly fat and unable to swim without little red water wings. In yet another lodge in our lane there was a French couple. They appeared to live in great simplicity if not poverty, always pleasantly dishevelled and seemingly eating little but rice. We were intrigued by their austerity – until we discovered that they were desperate to leave, but were prevented by the bus strike. Each morning they went up to the village to enquire at the bus office, but no, there were no buses. Finally they produced wadges of banknotes and American Express cheques and booked two seats on a chartered helicopter.

We looked at all these, and at ourselves.

One morning I embarked on another long walk, setting off as soon as the rain eased. I reached the distant tea shop, and one of my young acquaintance pulled me inside. The same beautiful girl was serving; she was his sister, he said, nineteen years old and unmarried. I glanced at her – and again she retreated to the kitchen. Her brother watched all this carefully, then announced that he would walk with me because the paths were difficult and there were many serpents.

Certainly the way was awkward; one minute the mud had my feet slithering inside my sandals; the next I was crossing a spur of sharp scree. Faced with a river, I took off my jeans and waded, fearing for my passport. It was absurd to be traipsing around the countryside with everything precious in a pouch, but we feared disaster should we became separated from our documents. The boy was a Brahmin; he wore his identity on a string about his neck.

By the time we returned to the tea shop we were both carrying our trousers and our shoes, walking in our underpants with mud up to our thighs, pulling off the gobbets and throwing them into each other's hair. There at the back was Jagath the lakeland *rentier,* toasting himself some maize whose warm burnt scent made me salivate. My companion consumed all the tea and biscuits I could buy him, while Jagath gave me betel and offered to show me one of the houses he had for rent. We walked past fishermen's homes where long tube-nets hung out in the sun.

The house was on a hillock of its own, overlooking the lake. It was the usual red mud and thatch, but small, the bedroom reached by a notched bamboo ladder. There was a porch at the front where I could visualize a cowboy with his feet up on the rail, strumming a guitar. At the rear there was a lean-to kitchen with a stone fireplace. There was no plumbing or sanitation, only a stream and a capacious lake, with plenty of space and no clutter. All around the house the ground was deeply slashed by erosion gullies where chickens stabbed and scratched, with tangles of knotweed and a lovely view across the water to mountains beyond. It was mine for 120 rupees a month.

I said that I would like to come back next year.

'You will forget,' smiled Jagath.

It was time for a swim; we found ourselves sitting on a rock jutting into the water. My companion was sixteen and said that he was married to a fifteen year old girl. He had no pubic hair whatever, and he swam ineptly. When we had landed and shaken ourselves dry, he declared that he had three proposals for me. Firstly, I should marry his gorgeous sister. Secondly, I should persuade Georgia that she should buy his trousers for R60, which was ten more than he'd paid for them. He assured me that, if I talked Georgia into this, he and I would go on a sweetmeat tour of Pokhara. Thirdly, I should buy him a curry because we were both cold and he was suffering from TB. At this, I decided that he was a mercenary little sod. I left him at his mother's tea shop, accepted a few puffs of something in a small wooden pipe, and squelched off in a cross daze. With this, I lost all desire to stay long among the lovely mountains, a parasite and a prey to parasites.

At the lodge, we went to the kitchen looking for an evening meal. Although we sat at a wooden table right at the front door, we could not see in, because inside it was pitch black regardless of the time of day. There was no chimney; the smoke seeped out of the thatch as though from a wet garden bonfire. A smiling but silent woman would sometimes emerge with plates of porridge or noodles, stodgy pancakes or a dinner of vegetable curry, raw onion, dhal and an awful lot of rice. The crudely printed menus were a precious genre: our lakeside lodge offered us 'dopple scrombow oggs' and 'gramet gustard' (caramel custard). Tonight, we could smell these things – but could only afford the porridge. Angela had done her sums again. She declared that we had not enough money both to pay for our room and to eat tomorrow unless Georgia pulled off the sale of some clothing for which the manager had offered her R20. I had by mistake left one of my Afghan shirts at the hospital with Dr and Mrs Bartholomew, and speculated: would they change some money for me? And suppose I was to go there at lunchtime and fetch it, would I get some more of their excellent bread and buffalo cream? I had no business complaining about parasites.

We had been travelling almost a month. In that time, I had spent all of £30, and a note in my diary says: 'We're increasingly miserly; I calculate that I have $28 a week left to me, which is a lot.' But just now we were running out of cash. We had enough rupees for one more dinner.

In the morning we dragged our loads to a room in the Yak Guesthouse in Pokhara village, ready for an early bus to Kathmandu; the strike was over. Angela walked very slowly, saying that her kidneys were hurting. She and Georgia flopped onto their beds, so I set out for the Shining Hospital, my brain saying 'This is really cheap' while my stomach questioned whether I had the timing right for lunch. I walked quickly, light-headed with hunger, while absurdly incongruous associations fixed themselves in my mind: the slow, slow plodding of buffaloes had me humming the opening bars of Vaughan Williams' G Minor Mass, while small boys on bicycles reminded me of Maçiek dying on a rubbish dump at the end of *Ashes & Diamonds*. As I passed up through the village, a convoy of military trucks passed through, several hundred soldiers heading towards the mountains. The villagers stared and murmured.

The Bartholomews sat in the kitchen. They happily exchanged some dollars for rupees, I found my shirt and accepted a glass of lemonade. A tense moment. The two small children sat opposite me finishing their lunch lingeringly. My empty stomach threatened to groan in protest, like Humphrey Bogart's in *The African Queen*. I told Dr Bartholomew that Georgia was studying at Clare College, Cambridge.

'How do you mean?' he asked.

'That's where she's reading English.'

'But Clare is a man's college.'

'Not now. Nor is King's. They're co-residential.'

'Good Lord,' said the doctor, glancing at his wife. 'It's been a long time...'

'Will you stay for lunch?' she asked. 'Just some rice and stuff.'

'Well...'

'It's nice to hear about things.'

'Oh dear, I do feel a parasite.'

I'd been practising the intonation of that all the way up the hill.

As I ate, I mentioned the trucks of soldiers.

'They're going after the Khampas,' said the doctor, 'an army of refugee Tibetan tribesmen in the hills, people who led the '59 revolt against the

Chinese. But the Chinese give Nepal a lot of aid, and they don't take kindly to being raided across the border. And the Khampas have made themselves unpopular in Nepal of late. Their CIA money dried up, so they've started stealing from villages and abducting local women.'

'Is this why there's a ban on trekking at the moment?'

'Heavens, yes. If you went trekking now you'd get yourself shot. The Khampas won't be easy to subdue; there's several thousand of them, and they know the mountains as well as the Nepalese. They are far to the west in Mustang; the terrain is extremely difficult, no roads anywhere near. The soldiers will have to walk for two weeks just to get close. It's taking the Nepalese ages to prepare. So far they've only got about eight hundred soldiers up there. A battle would be a desperate business.'

I thought of the Gurkhas I'd seen in the trucks, their kukris at their belts. A friend in Britain once gave me one of those knives; I almost took a finger off with it, hacking at an Oxfordshire elder bush. Many years later, when I wrote my first novel concerning the Chinese invasion of Tibet and the Khampa resistance, I remembered those trucks of soldiers heading west to finish off the last Tibetan army.

I had been steadily devouring coffee and flapjacks as the doctor talked – until Mrs Bartholomew removed the tin and firmly replaced the lid. I blushed and said I should be going.

'Come and see the hospital,' said the doctor. 'This is the best place in the world to study TB. Everyone has it, and often advanced. We are the westernmost hospital in Nepal, at the end of the highway. Further west – where the Khampas are – there's nothing but hill paths for two hundred miles: one hell of a walk if you're sick. So they don't bother until they're really bad.'

Under the shining tin roof, I thought of the boy by the lake, wanting a good meal to counter his TB, and how I'd dismissed him. Doctor Bartholomew said.

'Your friend Eric was a prize waste of time, if you'll forgive my saying so. He sat by the lake smoking marijuana half the day and the rest of the time was quite useless. He could have learned things here.'

He was thoroughly irritated by the likes of Eric.

'I've never met him,' I said, blaming Eric on Angela.

As a shower rattled on the tin roof, the doctor gazed around the isolated world he knew so intimately and had given his life to. I did not want to be either a lonely saint or a waste of time. Twelve years later, however, when I was a tropical diseases nurse in the forests of Burma, I would lie awake in my hammock at night considering both my delight in strange circumstances, and my loneliness.

I walked back through the village and discovered the whereabouts of the redundant traffic policeman seen by Robert Byron in Herat, Afghanistan, in 1933: he'd been transferred, he was here in Pokhara. He stood on a white pillbox in the middle of the only intersection in town, watching and waiting. There were no cars at all, but if a bus came anywhere within range a fearful shrilling of the policeman's whistle and a vigorous semaphore left the bus driver in no doubt that he would go in the direction in which he'd always intended to go anyway, which he did. Bicycles were more problematic, since the policeman had his dignity and doubted whether bicycles merited his attention. A half-hearted peep and a baleful glare were all that bicycles got.

Newly flush with the doctor's cash, I drifted down the street sampling every sweetmeat on offer, every combination of milk, flour, sugar, buffalo cheese and ghee, simmered down for hours in wide, shallow pans and sprinkled with rosewater or nuts.

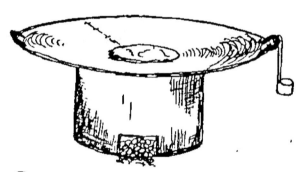

Boiling down milk on a charcoal stove.

The shops were open-fronted and the confectioner stirred in full view of a critical public. The surrounding street was thick with the scent, the

92

sweet's best advertisement. I should have been content with the scent; one blend of ghee, sugar and cheese tasted very like another.

Nor was there much variety in other food: rice, mild curries, dhal, buffalo meat, noodles and onions, all oddly tasteless and requiring plentiful soy sauce. To entice the travellers, they also offered omelettes, lemon juice, porridge and cocoa, fruit salad and yoghurt, and vegetable samosas. It was a menu that was available across Asia; here, much of it was trucked in from Kathmandu. As I descended past a school, an assistant master, standing in the doorway of his class, charmingly offered me a cold crumpet stuffed with goat cheese, with molasses dribbled over it.

In the post-shower freshness, Pokhara came alive. On the cracked paving stones below our window in the Yak Guesthouse, a knot of porters – each with a sack to protect his back from loads – were watching the Kathmandu road; they were waiting for their pay, so that they could set off home with provisions. There were shrines everywhere, standing on stone slabs in front of a house, a tree or a sweetmeat shop, some like clay balaclava helmets three or four feet high, some with slender carved stone pillars flanking the entry, with a brass bell dangling and a smudge of dyes and pastels. In front of one shrine sat a young scholar patiently transcribing fine calligraphy from an old volume into an exercise book. On a small knoll under a tree, another shrine doubled as a school where the children were being given a singing lesson: a steady chant of sixths, up and down, *do la do la do* – as though extolling the fat princeling flapping his water wings in slow motion down in the lake. A funeral trotted past with no more fuss than a bread delivery; four men carried an orange draped corpse on a rough wooden stretcher, three more jogging behind with bundles of firewood. No one paid them the slightest attention. The populace was dressing up; the manager of The Yak said that there was a festival starting tonight. The women had fetched out their finest saris, spectacularly gaudy against the rain-streaked cement walls. The older men were scented, and dressed in white. The young swells of Pokhara had on their snappy trousers and tailored shirts; I saw one printed all over with Great Bridges of the World, another with squash racquets and black balls. Bizarre and brash in well-heeled, pointed and highly polished shoes, they were trapped by their finery, and for fear of mud could not stray beyond the few hundred yards of metalled road. The porters below my window – browns and ochres, faded greens and dark gold skins – paid them no attention. The festivities were to start at midnight. It was raining hard, and I hoped that the traffic policeman had gone home. From the dusk came menacing squalls of shawms and fusillades of drumming.

Georgia joined me on the balcony to watch. Out of nothing, she said:

'I feel like Malcolm Lowry.'

'Oh dear, I'm sorry. Why?'

'I'm lost.'

She did not elaborate.

Downstairs with Angela, I scanned the drinks menu.

'You bring me Ginger Napoleon.' (Why on earth did we speak like that?) 'No? OK, you bring me *anar*? You bring me *khus*? No? All finished? You bring me black tea.'

He brought me a cup of cocoa instead, made with thin powdered milk. The cocoa had not been mixed to a paste first, and skulked at the bottom of the cup.

Two buses arrived; before they'd stopped, boys swarmed up onto the roof and started unlashing the baggage. The passengers trembled with exhaustion and noise after a day on the road from Kathmandu and clambering across landslips in the rain. An Australian enthused:

'That's a really great road, you know? I mean, it's prestige, it's profile, this is *the* strategic country in this neck of the woods and nobody's going to be seen to be mean so the locals got their arses into gear and started dropping hints and, oh brother, these Nepalis are shrewd little cunts. That road has been built in ten kilometre sections and you can see the signboards: *This section donated by the People of the United States,* and *This section built by the crudding Russians,* or *Next ten kilometres built by the French.* They have just played the geography a treat.'

A Dutchman looked about him in fright, grabbed his girlfriend's rucksack and steered her into The Yak for an omelette and Coke.

'Kathmandu,' he said, 'is just like any other international city. This is the real Nepal.'

A photograph shows me back in Kathmandu; I'm resting on my sleeping bag spread out on a bed in a very cheap hotel, the De-Light Lodge. I'm

wearing my grey Afghan shirt, and my hair hangs in a heavy black mass
down the side of my head. I look extremely pleased with myself for having

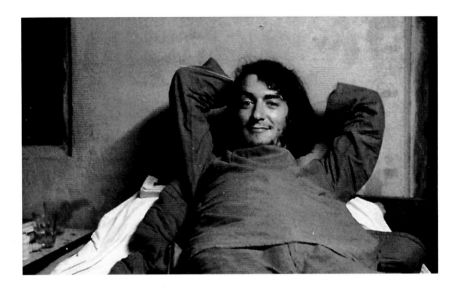

got here. Compared with the photograph taken in Cambridge that same
year, I look distinctly rough, but with the same cocky arrogance of youth.

I have another of Georgia and Angela side by side on a bed. Georgia
sits up straight, playing a part that she would affect from time to time: of
being faintly mad, eyes half obscured by her ginger curls and rolled
upwards like a dippy Baroque lady martyr. She wears a thin cotton shift
hanging from a halter string around her neck. Beside her is Angela, relaxed
and mountainous, gazing back at the camera with an ironic smile as though
about to ask a searching question. She is wondering when she will leave us,
but has not said so yet.

Trailing across India to find our flight to Nepal, Georgia had been
difficult and moody, complaining that we were leading her about by the
nose. She had hinted that we were scheming behind her back, and
maligning her. If asked her opinion about some plan, she'd snap:

'Oh for God's sake, don't ask me. I'm sure you've decided it all
between you already.'

I had seen Angela regard her with a quizzical expression that said: *How
long do I put up with this?* And I had realised that Angela would leave.

I had written in my diary:

'This is sad, because I love to see Angela shuffling enormously across Asia, delighted with everything. But Georgia is not to be abandoned. Her nerves would be undone within a week. She'd crumble, she'd go home.'

I do not now suppose that this was the case at all; Georgia was not the bravest of people superficially, and was easily alarmed by a buffalo or a snake. Still, she had her own dogged courage, and would not be deterred from anything. But I needed to be needed. And Georgia, consciously or not, had been driving Angela away.

And at last, Angela was decisive: on August 1st, she announced that she would be leaving us. She was heading for Sri Lanka to stay with British diplomatic contacts. It hardly seemed like the mountain landscapes and little villages she had so yearned for. She believed she had the journey calculated precisely: the flights, the trains, the ferries that would get her to Sri Lanka – a strange calculation for someone asking India to wash over her.

I would be alone with Georgia. I watched her as she pored over the map of India, and I imagined all the things we might see together, but also the length of time we would be in each other's constant company: a total of some seventy days, until at last we flew home from Bombay.

Kathmandu was not at all like any other international city: it was the most medieval place that I had ever seen. It was a very curious colour, as though the whole city was regularly sluiced with a clay-brown water, the sort of liquid that slithers off potters' wheels. It was a very faecal city. In De-Light Lodge our room was clean and the shower hot – but of a morning, I would step out into a dirt lane, to find that ours and every other backstreet was lined with squatting Nepalese, their pants about their knees, their excrement pale and liquid. As V.S.Naipaul wrote of India, it was a culture at once filthy and obsessed with purification. It was heaven and hell in one tiny town, a fantastic clutter of temples, shrines and wood carving, music and colour, shit and sordid poverty. It was thoroughly squalid – which was what made it seem truly medieval compared to those trim little towns on Tuscan hillsides. The temples were dissolving, subsiding brick by crumbled brick into the shitty streets. There was grass on the shrine roof, and a clutch of barbers below hanging towels from nails on the sacred door posts while they busily carpeted the temple steps with rotting human hair. Displaced masonry in the mud snagged my feet as I walked gazing up at the dark carved wooden grilles on every overhanging window. Many of these ancient windows had umbrellas dangling from them, upside down and open, forever drying.

There was one elaborate carved façade that I would pass when walking to and fro to De-Light Lodge. It was a building that seemed in slightly better repair than most. There was a tout on the door:

'See Living Goddess! See Living Goddess!'

Ah yes, her: chosen off the streets aged three or four, treated as a goddess until puberty, and then kicked out – and unlikely to marry because stories said anyone who married a former Living Goddess would die young. So she had to capitalise on the opportunity while it lasted. The tout wanted cash; he said he would pay the maidservants to bring the Living Goddess to a window overlooking the courtyard, to wave to me. Just at that moment, as I peered in through the gateway, a wooden grille slid open and there she was anyway, giving me a supercilious grin. Then she giggled and dived back into the gloom.

'You see! Now you pay! Living Goddess, yes!' cried the tout.

I shrugged and walked on. Such things seemed normal in Kathmandu.

'Live Breughel,' someone called it. I sat watching from the steps of a shrine in Durbar Square. Men sat playing cards on the temple steps, or had themselves shaved. A fruit seller with his barrow had erected an awning to keep off drizzle and sun, tying it to the Buddha's neck; there were posters advertising an Indian film stuck on the Buddha's back. (It reminded me of an incident in the career of John Donne, Dean of St Pauls; he'd caught a simple man urinating against a pier in the transept of the cathedral. The man said he was terribly sorry, he hadn't realised it was a church.)

Small boys were on the steps with me, flying fighting kites, the skyline sliced up by the glassy strings. The sound of bells was everywhere: prayer bells, bells shaken in procession, the soft clunk of big temple bells, the twitter of bicycle bells. Groups of men on cycles rode together like squadrons of cavalry, with jingling bells instead of jangling harness. Round the back of the shrine was an entrance; an old woman lived inside. She handed me a piece of card, saying:

> I am an old man.
> I have been the guardian of the shrine
> for twenty years
> I appeal to your honour to give me R3/-

In the gloom behind her was a fire with cooking pots and, on a round stone, a can of grapefruit segments and a transistor radio.

The city was disintegrating. A few grander buildings had scaffolding and UNESCO placards, but on all sides beautiful structures were disintegrating, leaving patches of mud and nettles. Everywhere was a thin, slithery mud that dried over one's shoes like the bloom on a plum; everything was always either drying out or getting wet again. In temple courtyards, pigeons smeared guano onto Buddha's nose while cockroaches fussed about on his arms, and lizards – the quintessence at once of stillness and flight – sat poised among the cows and the children and the incense holders in the courtyards. I walked through a warren of backstreets to come upon a river of whose existence I'd hardly been aware. The alleys were more Gothic than ever, claustrophobic and filthy but with a soft brown beauty also, the brick with all its mortar washed out leaving the walls scarcely solid. It was like a ghetto, a place for pogroms, the lair of some *mitteleuropäisch* horde of clockmakers. There was a narrow suspension bridge across the river, with bathing *ghats* and bolshy goats. By the bridge was an open space with a shrine and a tree which over the years had cracked and heaved up the paving slabs and threatened to topple the shrine. A cobbler with a box of tools leaned his back against the shrine while he showed a young boy how to trim surplus leather from a new heel. A monkey dropped from the tree, grabbed a sliver of leather and ran off across the suspension bridge, sucking it.

As dusk drew on, the curio sellers packed their trash away into tin boxes. At night the streets became stranger still, Chaucerian or fantastical.

There was little electric light anywhere. Wandering bemused after dark sometimes made me think of elaborate Hollywood film sets of ancient cities, except that no film ever matched this intricate squalor. In the market streets, pressure lamps lit caves inhabited by goblin-traders, their shops no more than cupboards at street level or below, into which you peered out of the darkness of the street into a rich box of treasures, of spices and sweetmeats, cloths and utensils which by daylight would look entirely mundane. The temples were lit by oil lamps which made the interiors hotter and more lugubrious than ever. Lights and scents and the ringing of small bells washed about me; I'd round a corner – and be obliged to jump into the faeces at the side of the street to avoid a line of jogging, taper-bearing, bell and cymbal-clattering, shawm-squealing saffron figures appearing out of the darkness. A bellowing drew me round a corner – and it was a monk giving a public scripture reading by lamplight. A drumming called me to the far side of yet another temple occupying the middle of the street, and there was a mob hurling coloured rice at a grimacing plaster goddess.

Georgia had been wandering too, alert and astonished, her eyes wide and drinking in the strangeness. In De-Light Lodge she tried to record everything, but could not write fast enough, and anyway wanted to be out again. She could not keep still.

Everything was weird, everything suggestive of a thousand associations and surprises. We were famished – but what did a Living Goddess eat? We picked our way cautiously through the unlit toilet street and past her window to find buffalo stew and curds for supper. Food as an obsession never left us: its cost, its palatability, its spiritual overtones, its hepatitis load. Food was a staple of travellers' talk. An American acquaintance from Pokhara re-appeared in Kathmandu; I found him buying old coins in the market from a barber who had half an eye on the American and half an eye on the cut-throat razor he was running over the throat of another customer.

'Yes indeed, sir, one thousand five hundred years old.'

'Really? Before the British, heh?' He bought two, then invited me to join him for a glass of lashi and pineapple.

'You know, I was in Pokhara last year,' he said, 'and there was no trouble with trekking. One time I went off on my own and I planned it really badly, so by the time I was coming down I was right out of food. When I came to a house I was pretty desperate so I went right up to the door and knocked. When a woman came out, I held out some rupees and pointed to my mouth. Well, they were eating right then, so I went in and sat down on a stool, and there was dad and three little kids and they had one big bowl of this grey gruel and they were all sitting around shovelling this slop into their mouths and all slobbering into it and I just couldn't. I had to point at a fry pan and get them to make me some little cakes.'

Most reliable were the 'pie and chai' shops. All across Asia, whenever the going was hard, I'd cheered myself up with thoughts of apple crumble – and in Kathmandu you could buy the most exquisite apple crumble. Pie and chai shops were run by ex-Gurkha families, who had learned how to make every sort of fruit and custard pie from the British. There was an excellent one along the lane from the De-Light Lodge, and I'd slip out for a little something before bed. 'I knew that's where you'd be going,' Georgia would remark, not disdaining the Danish cinnamon cake I'd brought her.

One afternoon, I was approached by a hard-eyed young German, very direct in his approach:

'You have any change?'

'What do you want to change?'

'Money for eating, please. I have 45 *paise* only.'

I gave him five rupees. He hardly bothered to nod his thanks and stalked off to the nearest pie shop. There was a one-legged Nepali whom I'd often seen begging near the De-Light Lodge; I'd never given him anything – only to a perfectly healthy and rather uncivil European. Two days later, I again met the German who did not recognise me because his hair hung over his eyes.

'You have any change? I have 45 *paise* only and I want money for eating, please.'

'That's what you said two days ago.'

'What?'

'You asked me for money two days ago. You only had 45 *paise* then.'

'So I was hungry two days ago. It is not strange that I am hungry now.'

At this moment, an apple rolled across the street in front of us. An unusual fight had broken out. Two young men – one in the street with a barrow of fruit, the other leaning out of an ornate first floor window fitted with carved dragons and wooden grilles – were hurling apples and furious insults at each other. One fruit pulped itself on the carvings above; another scudded across the street into a drain. A third, hitting the fruit seller on the thigh, was that which had rolled in front of us. The German picked it up, wiped it down carefully, and walked away munching.

Everyone was obsessed with getting sick, and with some reason. Angela was amoebic and incontinent.

'I stand under the shower and turn it on, and the sensation of water running down me makes all the food just flow out.'

Most travellers kept to the travellers' restaurants where they felt safe, with food they knew. The diet in Kathmandu had engaging eccentricities; there was the usual selection of parathas, yoghurt and dopple scrombow oggs, but the speciality of town was chocolate porridge, made from Fry's Cocoa Powder and tinned Quaker Oats (produced a few miles from where I now live in Fife). The American who'd been unable to eat the farmers' gruel said:

'Jesus, I even eat that chocolate porridge shit. Is that something you British dreamed up? I eat that stuff every day.'

Chocolate porridge was served in every travellers' restaurant. We were discerning patrons, seeking out establishments that provided quality and quiet. Some were insufferable, full of bedraggled youth from London and Lisbon, Zurich and Quebec, in a penumbral atmosphere of sweet scented smoke and Pink Floyd. One was called Divine Light Diner, another Old Hungry Eye.

Eating an omelette in one such dive, I saw through the purple gloom a grubby sheaf of stencilled papers on the next table. It was the 'BIT Guide' to the East, which dictated to young travellers what they could, should or shouldn't do. It was very detailed, especially on the subject of buying dope:

> Beware the Sharma brothers. They'll give you first-class weed to sample, promise to despatch a consignment airmail, take your money and that's the last you'll see of them. If you get busted, Captain Anand is the man to bribe.

The proprietor fitted a tape of Bob Dylan into his cassette player, while a little child – four or five years old – carried in two more bowls of chocolate porridge and studied the clientele with impassive eyes.

One afternoon, I spent an hour savouring the air-conditioning of the U.S. Information Service library, and found an article in the Herald

Tribune in which some expert in Chicago threatened food shortages especially in India. He foresaw millions of dead. I mentioned this to Georgia and we both declared that we'd limit ourselves to one bowl of porridge morning and evening. It would save money, after all.

I had also found, in a magazine, a long poem by John Ashberry:

What is beautiful seems so only in relation to a specific life,
experienced or not...
Exist? Certainly the leisure to
indulge stately pastimes doesn't
any more.

Nepal was full of people trying to determine what was beautiful in relation to their lives. And there was no shortage of leisure, though the stateliness of the pastime was questionable. I asked my American friend:

'How did you manage to stay in Nepal for so long? We could only get visas for two weeks.'

'Oh, they'll extend if you ask nicely. I've got friends in the US Information. There are plenty of guys here who overstay; they sell their passports. Then when they want to go home they just report to the embassy and have themselves shipped back.'

'But don't they want to go on to India?'

'No way! Kathmandu is the end of the line.'

Others reappeared from along the line. In the post office, I met an Italian girl who had been in the next compartment on the *Van Golu Ekspresi* in Turkey; she was doing as I was: fishing for letters from home. There was an English girl from Oxfordshire, from a village not far from my own; she'd trained at the same teaching college as my sister. She'd come out to India sharing the costs in a minibus advertised in the New Statesman: £180 without food.

'I'd never travel that way again. I hardly met any locals, or anyone at all except the five other passengers, all the way from London to Delhi.'

Of an evening, vaguely familiar faces would be with me sitting on the steps rising up the side of the shrine in Durbar Square, half a dozen travellers gazing at the scene, and all looking the part: faded shirts and limp cotton skirts, straggly hair, half-closed eyes and silly smiles. It was not as though we even brought in much money, on our two bowls of chocolate porridge a day – but commercial drive did not seem too pressing in Kathmandu. In the tiny cave-like shops around Durbar Square, little was happening. Each shop was just big enough for one small and silent man who often sat with his back to the street, reading. A few of the caves were inhabited by lovely young girls, their thin faces with beautifully clean lines and strong dark eyes, sharper featured than north Indian women. One afternoon there seemed to be a schools or scouts event: graceful girls were out on the streets in saris of a pale brown with a peachy tinge, with white scarves and hair drawn neatly back. They looked stunning. We gazed at them and they gazed back at our uncouth begging, our chocolate porridge, our Led Zeppelin and our bribes and our astonishing freedom to come and go. Were we a cause of malaise, disgust or envy? We were utterly shabby.

There was one singular angst suffered by the travellers: whether or not to buy 'ethnic' clothing from the Tibetan refugees who lived in colonies around the edges of Kathmandu weaving for tourists. I came upon a bazaar in which a dozen temples were interspersed with stall on stall of 'Tibetan' coats and jackets made of rough hair, with brightly coloured woven strips along the seams. These were warm and comforting, but to dress in such things would be to follow the sheep – just what we had come East to escape.

I became addicted to the sights, like any tourist in London dazzled by the banalities of Oxford Street. I marvelled at the fabric shops and spice shops that made the streets pungent. Or the bead street, with acres of beads laid out on white sheets on the ground. And the hawkers of bamboo flutes held in a giant bottle brush arrangement, with a long pole resting vertically against their shoulder; as the man walked, the whole contrivance rattled while the man played another flute single handed.

From fifty yards, a tinsmith's shop festooned with rice boilers and saucepans, lamps and implements looked like the entrance to a shrine with door jambs of richly worked silver. I blundered into a courtyard, tiny and crowded with an elaborate gilded temple. All about the central shrine thronged scores of carvings: stone bells, gods, inscribed tablets, all set upright seemingly at random in the pavement, as though the precinct was an atelier. All the time there were processions coming and going, marching and counter-marching. Sometimes there would be monks, sometimes ordinary people with a couple of old clarinets, a trumpet and a few drums and cymbals, roaring and screeching and battering their way through the crowds with a plethora of umbrellas. Sometimes the processions ducked into the cramped temple courtyards, circled the shrines at a fast trot and then swayed raucously away along the street leaving the pigeons, rats and cockroaches of the temple to regroup cautiously in time for the next assault. And then, quite suddenly, around the corner came the procession of the Living Goddess borne in a litter surmounted by a dome of red cloth, dressed to kill in gold brocade and a crimson woolly hat with tassels dangling from the brim, carried by four men jogging with loud clashing of cymbals, barging through the shoppers and enjoying herself immensely, leaving a coloured ripple in the air as she passed.

To Patan, 'city of fine arts', a name calculated to fill me with terror. Architecturally, Patan made Kathmandu look like Woking. A town of concrete electricity pylons, herringbone brick streets and 1400 shrines. It was all too much for Georgia, who saw her favourite deity – Ganesha of the elephant trunk – at every turn.

I sat on the steps and stared vacantly ahead of me, wondering if E.M. Forster ever wrote 'On Not Looking at Temples'. In a dutiful frame of mind I spent an hour in a museum full of Buddhist bronzes which the Nepalese had been manufacturing for the Tibetans for centuries. I did not come to love them. I could not stop thinking of an old Giles cartoon of a family at an auction finding themselves lumbered with an unbelievably hideous brass Hercules lamp stand because their small boy had ostentatiously blown his nose on a large white hanky.

Besides which, I was being trailed by the custodian, a young man in a red lumberjack shirt. He maintained a few precisely measured paces behind me. If I moved, he moved the same number of steps, forward or back, silent on soft soles. I plotted to take one sudden jump backwards onto his toes.

Much more to my taste than the bronzes were the portraits of the kings of Nepal, a long row of these, each with a reverent biography underneath. The custodian found these very dull; I could hear him sighing with irritation as I read them all, increasingly delighted:

> In His Majesty Mahendra the qualities of leader of men, poet and philosopher were profoundly mingled.

The photograph showed a man with a puffy face. I wondered if he could swim, or if he used water wings. In each monarch the qualities were profoundly mingled, but in different combinations. I turned to the custodian:

'In my country we have had some very bad kings. Have you ever had bad kings in Nepal?'

He gave an embarrassed laugh and looked away a moment, before pulling himself together and saying:

'You see, sir, my country of Nepal is the only Hindu state never conquered by foreign power. So we have unique culture.'

'So I've heard. But what about your kings in the past? Have they all been wise men?'

'Sir, no king who knows about religion is a bad king.'

'So have all your kings been religious men?'

'Nepalese kings have all been very good. You can see,' he waved a hand round the museum, 'our king has given us this.'

He walked apart from me, looking scornful. I had learned nothing.

I went out, breaking my food resolve when faced with hot fried spinach cakes. I walked to the edge of town, and every child that I passed smiled and chanted, 'Hello! One rupee!'. It became quite appealing, and I found that if I simply smiled and chanted 'Hello! One rupee!' back in the same singsong tone it set them skipping in great good humour. They followed me into a courtyard full of bronze monsters scattered about on pedestals, mostly engaged in snarling at something. The children continued to play, but quietly, not wanting to attract the beasts' attention. Several sat watching me writing and sketching for a quarter of an hour or more. When I walked around the courtyard photographing the monsters, three urchins followed me in file pretending to be pointing and clicking the same beasts.

I had been alternating *Don Quixote* with a new acquisition: Thomas Mann's *Magic Mountain,* in which I found this:

> Is the pastness of the past not the profounder, the completer, the more legendary the more immediately before the present it falls?

When I thought back to Afghanistan, it was like that; I was quite certain that I'd never go there again.

I stopped for a cup of tea. A young man was reading a newspaper.

'Good afternoon, sir, and welcome.'

'Thank you. This is a remarkable town.'

'A remarkable town, yes, sir. Did you know, sir, that Patan was once an independent state? This was not the same country as Kathmandu. Have you seen the museum of bronzes?'

'I saw it today. I liked the portraits of the kings of Nepal.'

'Good men, sir, all the people know that they are good men. King Birendra is so very popular. When he goes into the villages, the people worship him, sir, like a god, indeed *just* like a god, with prayers and with garlands of flowers. But he is not like a god because he works here on earth, with us the people. You see this palace?' He pointed to a large, ornate building across the road. 'Now it is the police station. Our kings are most practical.'

He gave me a half-hour disquisition on the virtues of Nepalese *panchyat* non-party democracy, which (I had no idea) was just then beginning to fall apart. He insisted on paying for the tea and the bread for dunking – which had a strong, earthy taste – and on escorting me back to the Kathmandu bus, which contained this plaque:

DIWAN COACH BUILDERS
BODY BUILDERS TO
STATE GOVERNMENTS

Georgia had some very intense days. She went off one morning to the 'monkey temple', the big stupa with creepy eyes that stares down from a hill on the edge of the city. On her return she tried to describe it, but tied herself in verbal knots and then became cross at my lack of understanding. Abandoning this, she began to teach herself to play the new bamboo flutes that we had bought, making slow progress. I pompously suggested that she learn more methodically, not attempting elaborate tunes before she could make a clean sound. It was a mistake; she became touchy, and began writing in her diary straight away.

Some days later, in a better humour, she took me to the monkey temple. At the top of the long hot climb was a confusion of curio sellers, cold drinks, scavenging dogs, pigeons and monkeys, and expanses of some variety of seed – beige and dusty, rather beautiful – laid out in the sun to dry, with an old woman flapping the pigeons off. Around the big central stupa was a ring of thousands of prayer-wheels; four middle-aged women were walking round and round running one hand over the wheels to keep then turning and churning out prayers, chanting all the while and shaded from the sun by parasols. Ripples of drums and bells came and went, and the painted eyes of the stupa looked headachy. Georgia led me from this to that: the shrines, the monks' quarters, the views of the city, showing me all that she had found. But then she said:

'You look so out of place in temples, Jo.'

So I moved out of the precinct, and sat on the steep grass with my trousers rolled, soaking up sun in lieu of anything else. Georgia stayed inside, drawing.

After Angela left us to fly south, we began to treat each other more carefully, faced with weeks at each other's mercy. Georgia bought a pretty rust-coloured skirt which set off her hair nicely; I liked to see her drift from street to street, nosing into everything, endlessly curious, wonderfully syncretic in her associations of ideas. She was changing; she had caught first hints of what she was after, and her tetchiness was turning to excitement.

So we schemed and planned together. We had a handful of contacts and addresses in India, and she wrote to one:

'We shall be wandering from Benares to Delhi by way of... please forward mail to... this is all very vague.'

Which was not the whole truth; we were working out the itinerary minutely. I couldn't see Georgia as 'wandering'; she was not a free agent in loose white wraps with a small cotton bag over her shoulders, hitching rides on bullock carts from village to village. Georgia was too curious, too changeable, too anxious, eager for new experiences but wary of immersion, just as she longed to soak herself in sun but knew her red colouring would burn. It all suited me. I had no illusions that I was there for a spiritual experience; I just wanted to see. I did not want to be a gentle spirit by the lake slowly wearying of my lover and their bicycle, still less a paper-less freak waiting to be repatriated.

Almost the last thing I saw in Kathmandu was the Union Jack Pub. It was a bar in one of the hotels, and displayed ancient photographs of the British Royals: George V's Durbar of 1911; the coronation of Edward VII; young Elizabeth with baby Charles. There was no bitter, but for two rupees one could have a shot of **KAT 29** whisky, locally made, with an oddly familiar label of white stencilled letters on a black ground. There was not much custom in the Union Jack Pub; the jacks were moth-eaten, and a dusty atmosphere hung there like an ageing expatriate, and that was the very last thing I wanted to be.

Georg Simmel wrote:

> The adventure, in its specific nature and charm, is a form of experiencing. The content does not make an adventure… In general, only youth knows this predominance of the process of life over its substance.

It was time to get to grips with India.

FIVE

SMALL EPISODES OF VIOLENCE

The adventure is that incomparable experience which can be interpreted only as a particular encompassing of the accidentally external by the internally necessary.

Georg Simmel

PATNA TRAIN,
Nr. KANPUR.

112

In the Patna-Gaya train I had a wooden shelf all my own to doze on, and an ineffectual fan by my ear. Everything in the carriage was either dark stained wood or painted a dull, clammy cream. From the windows, watching the countryside was like surveying a calm sea from a ship: change came about slowly in a dead flat landscape, mile on mile of paddy and grass and scrub. The train stopped here and there at small stations, just for a chat or to pick up beggars. Cripples worked the railway; they would drag themselves on board at one halt, beg their way from carriage to carriage along the line, then get off and wait for another train to take them back. Often they came in pairs. Sometimes they were young men, and blind; they would grope their way along the carriage moaning their prayers, four milky eyes skewed at frightful angles.

We bought an omelette from an attentive waiter who, in the quiet train, enjoyed the chance to be courteous. He asked our opinion of the omelette; it was a good omelette but we said that in our opinion it was over-priced. The waiter nodded thoughtfully; he agreed, and he would be obliged if we would write a letter to the Railways Board. He fetched a sheet of headed paper and between us we composed our letter.

A circle of educated gentlemen closed in on us. They wanted to know everything about British universities, about prices and marriage customs, and what we knew of India. Georgia and I had decided that, as our defensive relationship of the day, we would be half-brother and sister. A shrewd-looking Brahmin sitting directly opposite us, who had not spoken so far but had simply scrutinised Georgia's red hair, said suddenly:

'I do not think you are brother and sister.'

'Half-brother and sister,' I corrected.

'I do not think you are half-brother and half-sister.'

'Oh. Why's that?'

'Because you are not looking alike.'

'Ah, but in England brothers and sisters often don't, you see, it's a genetic thing...'

The Brahmin smiled a faint indulgent smile, and I felt all the chagrin of having dug myself into a deep hole. Whose idea had that been? Why could we not simply be friends?

I took against one of these gentlemen, a fat slob with greasy, sweaty skin, flesh oozing out of every seam of his clothes, given to leafing through our Fodor with uncouth paws that threatened to tear out every page, while leering at Georgia. I wondered whether I should take umbrage. What if we had pretended to be married? I thought of Levin in *Anna Karenina,* taking disproportionate offence at a guest's flirtation with Kitty and throwing him off the estate. That's what I should have done.

But of course the slob was the most generous and articulate of all. He stopped every vendor who passed down the train, buying us cigarettes and nuts and sweetmeats, telling us the names of each, how they were made and sometimes a little story of their origins.

One of them asked me to recite some Wordsworth. They all examined my passport, calculated my age and expressed amazement at my beard, and then demanded to know when and whom I would marry, nodding questioningly towards Georgia who was turning scarlet.

'She is my half-sist…'

'Yes. We hope you will marry soon.'

As the train slowed into Gaya station and they all reached for their bags, a dapper civil servant apologised for 'engaging' us for so long.

Further reminders that we were back in India: the heat, the crowds, the people sleeping on the platforms, and a cow curled up contentedly in the second class waiting room. Also, the uncertainties dogging every attempt at planning: at the bus station we asked about services to Bodh Gaya – could we get there tonight? An official assured us that we could. His colleague disagreed. We tried a third, who wasn't sure. A fourth was definite that we could not; the last bus to Bodh Gaya, as shown on the timetable, left at 4.25 p.m. which was ten minutes gone. Walking resignedly out of the terminus we were almost mown down by a bus – the last bus to Bodh Gaya, leaving late.

In the Rest House Terminus the manager was a caricature guru: long locks, white robes, much fingering of beads. You should not move about so much, he told us; remain in Gaya, become familiar with it. Outside, everything had a gleaming whiteness in the pale late afternoon light: white cars, white shirts, white cows. Beyond the tracks, the countryside was a gorgeous rampage of emerald greens, mud and palm trees. But do not walk out there after dark, said the manager, for fear of robbers.

We were going to Bodh Gaya, where the young Gautama Siddhartha had sat under the pipal tree and hoped for enlightenment. We got up at 5.30 a.m. in order to arrive in the cool before 7.30, and there were on the bus a number of serious-minded, educated and courteous men also going to the shrine. Dressed in flowing whites, they moved and spoke with their

unfussed gracefulness. There was also a group dressed in orange, each with a smart camera tucked among the folds; I had the idea that they were Burmese.

Bodh Gaya was quiet; even the village on the sidelines was quiet, though people busied themselves chivvying their goats and children, and pulling their bedding out for an airing.

Then something unforeseen happened to me. The enormous central shrine burst up through the trees, and I shuffled about the courtyard, then walked in and stood before the huge gilt image a moment. I climbed the steps through the temple's midriff and came out onto a high terrace where there was still shade from the tall trees and I could sit with my feet cool and my hands cool upon the stone, looking down on a crowd of men

weeding between the stone slabs in the courtyard below. After some time resting there, I dropped down through the interior again and came into a side temple with three large figures of the Buddha waiting in the half-dark. I sat down again on a small ledge, the cool sousing me. A monk came in behind me. After a moment or two of not moving, he took my hand and pulled me towards the large central image, touching my fingers first to the gilding, then to my own forehead, saying a prayer as he did so. He released me, and I returned to the ledge and looked back at the statue, resenting its closed eyes. By now I had almost ceased to think, and was aware only of the cool and of being surrounded by sleek gilt lines, and that my eyes were watering. I saw my companion regarding the image with his head held admiringly on one side. And then I felt the presence of despair – not that I had it, but that it was there, in what was otherwise an emotional void. I sat weeping, and it occurred to me that I was paying attention to myself in that condition, sitting in a dark chamber with three statues and a monk, tearful about a vacuum, and that I found the spectacle agreeable.

I retreated to a tea-shop, and felt more secure behind a table. After a while I felt safer; I felt that I had been warned of the vicinity of something that I categorically did not want, something that I disdained, something that Georgia might have welcomed, but not me. Feeling stronger, I went out again and sat under the tree, the Bo Tree, the very one under which Gautama Buddha received enlightenment, so they were telling me. All those years ago. Well!

There was a nice museum of archaeological finds where I sat and drew a foolish female divinity on a pillar, and made her look even sillier, to the great delight of the attendant. Outside, there was a huge lily pond with a bathing *ghat*. People kept coming and sitting by me for a moment or two – ordinary, earthbound people; they would exchange pleasantries and give me their addresses in Nagoya or Rangoon, and we would assure each other of a welcome.

Then a matrimonial fracas exploded nearby, on the grass by the Thai monastery. One faction of a large Indian family sided with a woman in a brilliant mauve sari, while the others sided with what I took to be her husband, at whom she howled and screeched until at last she flew at him with fists whirling, and chased him around the museum with forty relatives in pursuit.

I looked about for Georgia, my half-sister whom I must marry soon. There was an acre of white tombs, and among them Georgia drifted. But the tombs were populated by scores of large lizards which alarmed her; she came scampering back to the Bo Tree. She was happy pottering and examining everything, regaining her courage and returning to the smaller tombs, but warily, for fear of snakes. She looked beautiful in her russet skirt and an embroidered cream smock with a hood which she wore up against the sun, and out of which long curls of hair waved – a gathering of colours going among the white stones and rough green grass. She had a defiantly un-sensual manner of moving, a reluctant stoop which filled me with affection for her. She hated to be watched, fearing that she looked graceless, and reacted by stalking about with a deliberate (but faintly apologetic) further lack of grace that was curiously charming.

Walking back to the bus, we were nearly trampled by two elephants fitted with harness and chains for dragging logs. Beyond them, across a ravine lay a landscape of paddy and palm groves, then a river, high hills and a brilliantly lit apocalyptic cloudrack being drawn over the scene by cords of lightning. I bought some peanuts off a barrow. I thought them very expensive, and accused the man of doubling his prices for tourists. He looked hurt: I realised that I had confused quantities, and I apologised weakly. When the bus was moving and I opened my twist of peanuts, I found that they were blighted and bitter, every one of them. Which was, I supposed, why the onlookers had been laughing.

Our first taste of the Railway Retiring Room: cheap, spotlessly clean, furnished with twin four-posters and ample mosquito nets, and complete with a private bathroom and a fan to stir the heat a little. The fittings well-rubbed but solid quality in the timber and tiling, and nothing altered in fifty years; one could imagine journeying District Commissioners and their mems taking their rest. But we got little sleep. It was like trying to doze inside the mechanism of a gigantic clock; the station clanked and roared in our ears. We had to be up before dawn for a train to Benares, so we retired early to our four-posters, lying naked on the crisp white sheets waiting for the porter to wake us at 4.45 a.m.

After drifting off briefly, I woke and fretted about the noise and the time. I peered out of the window and thought it might be about 4 a.m. There was a window overlooking the station also, and I stood there naked in the dark room, gazing down at the platforms and the changing lights of the railway. Georgia was awake also but not speaking; she opened her eyes and regarded me through the mosquito net.

I had no watch. Unable to bear the thought that it might be time for the train, I dressed and went downstairs to look at a clock: it was ten to eleven.

So I went out of the station, and was taken by storm. There were the crowds of daytime, but it was a different town, a filthy nightmare lit by nauseating pools of livid whiteness from neon tubes, and smudges of rancid yellow from oil lamps. I did not recognise anything. My disgust started in the station itself. The sleeping poor were everywhere; they'd flocked in for the night and lay packed side by side in the station foyer. In some places they lay still under their sheets, but in some places they were wriggling like monstrous grubby white larvae. A memory came to me of photographs of the corpses of Russian peasants left in the snow by the Wehrmacht, and of the stunned faces of the Russian soldiers who had found them. The whole station approach was carpeted with people, only a narrow passageway remaining, just enough for carts and cars whose wheels rolled over the edges of the sleepers' drapes, close to feet and hands. I began to pick my way out of the forecourt. Just beyond the gates were two small stages with figures of Krishna, tinselly and garish like a bad nativity crib, lit by neon tubes. A man shouted – *Birthday! Krishna's birthday!* – and waved a collecting tin at me. Music distorted beyond understanding shrieked out of a record player perched on the roof of the stage.

There were people everywhere, and all in constant movement. Even the thin men with piles of blackened bananas on the pavement continually jumped up and down to scream at each other. I went in search of somewhere to sit with an earthenware cup of tea and a rice cake, which had been 40 *paise* on the train; no one here would part with anything for less than 80 *paise*. I walked away from the station, spattering my trousers with rainwater, feeling feverish and heady, dodging the rickshaws that

120

came out of the darkness at me, my estimation of speed and distance thrown into disarray by the uneven light from scores of small oil lamps on sweetmeat stalls. The shops, all in full swing, were besieged by beggars who crawled off the streets across the crumbling paving stones to cling to the steel shop gates and whine, the braver ones creeping slowly into the shop itself to be paid off or – literally – kicked out.

Everywhere in the street, sweet milky tea boiled in urns alongside platters of stacked glutinous sweetmeats. There were men rolling *beedi* cigarettes and tying them into bundles of twenty with coloured cotton, women with lice in their hair who swayed towards me, waving tin bowls and screeching at me – *Sahib!* – and rickshaws and steaming kettles and walls of noise, men bellowing to each other from the tea stalls, shouting men on bicycles, a surge of undirected movement through which I lurched from one pool of light to the next.

At last, I turned back to the station after mistakenly buying a whole kilo of rice cakes for ten rupees. There in the hot Retiring Room, Georgia seemed to be asleep under her mosquito net, in just her small white pants, hugging the bolster. I stood gazing at her a while before gathering up the nylon folds of my net and creeping back inside.

A bearer hammered on the door at 4.45 a.m. precisely. In panic we both leapt out of bed and were washed, dressed and packed in five minutes. Then we rushed downstairs – I remember a broad stairway, with a dado of high-glaze dark green tiles – to buy our tickets. The train was very late; we could have slept another hour. We took our bags and our books and, for no obvious reason, went to different waiting rooms to read.

It was a good train, with a diesel-electric engine and no soot flying in through the window, and it took only five hours to cover the 130 or so miles from Gaya to Benares. We occupied two individual window seats, hoping to read in peace. But no Indian objects to standing over you in order to hold a conversation; we were trapped by a massive Punjabi who spoke poor English but who was determined to be our friend, to an extent that became alarming. He began by offering a cashew or two, highly spiced. He gave Georgia a saucer piled high with them. Then he revealed that he had a large cardboard box of sweetmeats, the most luxurious and costly varieties. He placed on the saucer two of the most succulent, wobbling and scented and oozing rosewater, and we ate them. Smiling, he replaced them, and we smiled and nodded our thanks and ate those too. He replaced them again, watching carefully to see how we smiled. We began to feel sick. His name, he announced, was Vipi.

The train stopped at Mughal Sarai across the river from Benares. Vipi and his companion got down from the carriage to order lunch – stainless steel platters of vegetable curries served from a large barrow with a built-in charcoal stove – which they tried to press me into accepting; I had stepped onto the platform, thereby putting their Punjabi honour to the test. All along the platform I could see the wealthier passengers standing by their carriages, holding their platters in one hand, eating with the other. Vipi's friend ate half of his, then gave the rest to a beggar couple with half a dozen children who divided it with scrupulous fairness, offering the platter to each other in turn. We were approached by a miserable woman, quite young, verminous and almost naked, whose stench rose even above the acrid oil smells of the train and the spices of the lunch barrow. The Punjabi led her off and bought her a plate of dhal and two chapatis. Vipi watched his friend for a moment, then said:

'Punjab rich, good state. This Bihar very poor state.'

He bought everyone tea, the beggar family and the woman too, keeping his distance from her while being gentle and courteous. Our tea came in cups with saucers; tea for the beggars was in little disposable clay mugs.

'You can't feed all of Bihar by yourself,' I said, as he seemed to be looking round for more hungry people. He smiled and replied:

'Sahib is a gentle person.'

I resolved to buy some chapatis for an old cripple who was watching us hopefully, but it seemed a grotesque sort of rivalry and I lost my nerve.

As the train approached the Ganges, he showed me on the map his home town of Maradabad. He owned a large brass foundry, he said, and wanted nothing more in the world than to show it to me. He would send me a brass gift to England. Whenever I returned to India, he would receive me at any airport.

We rumbled across the river. A knife-seller swayed down the corridor

122

and urged me to buy. He spoke no English, but persisted and persisted – so I took out my Norwegian sheath knife and bared my teeth. Thinking that it might amuse Vipi, I produced also my phallic folding Afghan knife and opened it – and at once my hand and arm were swarming with tiny ants. I'd cut a mango somewhere and had forgotten to wash up. My absurd arsenal was rapidly undermining my supposed gentleness. Vipi pretended not to notice, and placed the whole box of sweets on my knee where the ants soon found it. When the train finally stopped, Georgia climbed down with her rucksack and bought us a cold drink each. Vipi promptly leapt after her and insisted on paying for these, then tried to persuade us to accept a large fruit cake into the bargain. His friend called to him: the train was leaving.

'I am sorry to detain you. I will receive you at Delhi! You will not forget!'

We crossed a footbridge to leave the station. By the exit was the usual cluster of beggars. One of these, a teenage boy, stood behind an old man sleeping on the ground. I looked again: the old man's eyes and mouth were open, his head tilted strangely far back. His hands were tightly clenched. There were flies all over his face, walking in and out of his mouth.

'Sir, for funeral, money for funeral, sir.'

In May 1974, India had suffered the worst railway strike in its history; the 1.7 million railway workers were demanding an improvement on £15 a month for twelve hour shifts. They got no strike pay, thousands of strikers were arrested, and were cruelly penalised afterwards. We'd no idea of this.

Armed with student concessions, we went to the Benares stationmaster's office. Georgia's patience had gone for a walk. The official began by comparing heights; I was standing beside a tall Scandinavian.

'He is so much taller than you, and you are so much taller than me. I am so small!'

He joked with his friends and asked why I wasn't smiling on my student card. Georgia stalked out of the office in a fury, and he smiled at her retreating back.

'Your friend has no patience. Everyone must have patience, above all the railway worker.'

'Ah. Why the railway worker especially?'

'Because he must deal with an iron devil that will not wait. So, if he is not to be infected, he must practice patience and make a gentle spirit in himself.'

The Scandinavian guffawed sarcastically:

'Ja, you need patience because you must wait so long for the train to come.'

'No, sir! Now the trains are going very well. Better than ever they are running, because we have a strike.'

'Trains run better because of a strike?'

'So much better! First thing, when there is a terrible strike, all the passengers are scared there will be a bloodbath, so they are staying away, and the trains are empty and accommodating. Second thing, now the big strike is finished, all the workers are struggling to get back in favour with the foreman, so they work extra hard. It is wonderful to travel on the railway now.'

So it was.

We walked through the backstreets of Benares looking for a post-office, and were soon lost in lane after lane of squalor. We were jeered at for being self-indulgent tourists strolling in the stews. At last the heat overcame Georgia. She took to her bed in our rubbish hotel. Our ten rupee room was a hot little shack on the roof, full of ants, with a broken fan and a loudly dribbling shower next door. She lay naked and sweating, her sweat not evaporating at all. She was fading before my eyes.

I went out into the dark by myself. As I approached the Ganges, I was suddenly in a dangerous stream of rickshaws, scores of them and all unlit and undistinguishable one from another, jangling their bells furiously at anything that impeded their flow. Then a fruit market, and then a street full of stalls selling shimmeringly brilliant silks, shawls and saris, and wooden crates packed with incense.

Then the bathing ghats. The steps down to the river were jammed with rough wooden platforms, out of which tattered parasols grew so thickly together that they formed a roof over the steps. A Brahmin sat on each platform, waiting for spiritual clientele.

In the pressure-lamp light the parasols appeared to live, swaying and twitching – but that was the effect of the racing water behind them. Boatmen clamoured to offer me trips downstream, but the Ganges looked dangerous and uninviting. There was a mark on the wall showing the 1968 flood level, twenty feet above my head.

Lights burned upon the water, tiny straw boats with two wicks, which the bathers set upon the river with a prayer. It was late; there were few people bathing, two or three men in thin white cottons which billowed about them in the wind as they descended the steps, then clung wet to the legs. The gentlemen stepped gingerly into the flood, stirred the water to disperse the floating sewage, filled their mouths with Mother Ganges and squirted it quickly out again.

A glow came from the Burning Ghat downstream, the wind whipping sparks from the cremations into the black sky. I climbed up to a small

shrine jutting over the water, leaned out and listened to the darkness. An enormous, deep swelling rumble came over the water to me on a gust of wind that simultaneously lashed the cremation pyres and sent fire streaming across the boiling river. The sound grew louder still: a train was crossing the long iron bridge from Mughal Sarai.

The street lights failed as I walked back to the hotel, and my ears and eyes strained for clues. I could see very little. Suddenly a massive bulk swayed out of the gloom at me, and passed almost overhead, scattering rickshaws in panic. It was a camel. I groped my way home to find Georgia writing letters by candlelight.

I sat in the front room of the crummy hotel and ordered breakfast from the manager, another guru-figure in robes and beads. I discarded a few leaves of *Don Quixote,* then reached for a newspaper which was full of brief reports, each given minimal space, of outbreaks of startling violence. A train packed with delegates to a youth congress had stopped at a station. Some of the students had got into an argument with a tea vendor on the platform; other vendors had come to his aid. The result: a riot, with four people shot dead by the police. Four column inches.

Another headline:

SEVEN LANDLESS TILLERS FIRED UPON BY LANDLORDS

It had a curious demented quality to it, even while reminding me of the Seven Men of Knoydart who staged Scotland's last land raid in 1948. I showed this report to the guru-manager, and remarked how very little it took to provoke an incident. I said that I'd once read a Victorian theory about people who – like the Prussians – lived in areas of sandy soil and were more aggressive and prone to outbursts of violence, and I asked if he thought the soil, the climate or the Indian diet had anything to do with it.

> The innkeeper who was a shrewd fellow and already suspicious of the disorder in his guest's understanding, was fully convinced of it when he heard him talk after this manner.
>
> *Don Quixote*

He gave me a hard stare.

'India is the best country, the very best country. But nowhere is there

126

so much corruption and dishonesty. Even the beggar is not a true man. In his own home the beggar is a rich man who drinks whisky.'

I told him of the corpse at the station, and the son begging money for a decent burial.

'Pah! He was not dead. These Indians will do anything. At the highest levels everything is corrupt. Many people – and I count myself amongst them – say that there is only one hope for India, and that is military rule.'

I read more of the newspaper:

- Schoolmaster killed by parents disappointed at exam failures.
- Forty-five Congress Party MPs to be allocated free land for building houses in New Delhi. Angry minister confirms legality of grant.

They brought me a breakfast of vegetable parathas and tea; then we left the manager to his indignation and moved hotel.

Green Lodge is still there today, although in the website photos the décor is a lurid pink. In 1974 it was still green, quiet and pretty. We had a room with three French windows, our own shower, a variable speed fan, a writing table and a cool tiled floor. The hotel was built around a courtyard, and from our second floor balcony we could look down onto the family cooking, washing linen, playing with their children. We bought ourselves a bottle of fruit juice and some mangoes, deloused ourselves and washed everything, our bodies and the entire contents of our rucksacks. I carefully wrapped the rings I'd bought in Kabul in pages of *Don Quixote,* and we felt at home.

To the Burning Ghat in a late afternoon downpour. As we left Green Lodge, a cosmic bucket was upended over Benares; the street disappeared in moments under four inches of water. Everything stopped dead in its tracks. The rickshaw boys cowered under their hoods, and the din of rickshaw bells was turned off as though at a switch, to be replaced by the roar of rain. I pulled on my anorak and tried to dodge from doorway to doorway, but the rain drove straight through the waterproof. I was trapped by the rising flood, tried to balance on some broken bricks, missed my footing and went in.

As the waters subsided, we crept down tiny alleys packed with silk stalls and spice stalls that crushed inward from both sides to squeeze us until the money popped out. We asked for the Burning Ghat and were sent a dozen different ways, stumbling in confusion through the maze, alarmed and fascinated, until at last my normally excellent sense of direction failed and Georgia crowed in triumph.

Every Hindu aspires to be cremated on the Manmandika Burning Ghat, a prosaic concrete platform above the river. On the street nearby was a large pile of firewood. On the platform, ten pyres cremated in rotation, some smouldering, others blazing. Two had recently gone out and were being rebuilt for a new corpse wrapped in white. As one man bent down to light the kindling, another unceremoniously dumped more logs on top of the cadaver which shifted in protest. The flames caught and spread; a halo formed about the deceased, steam and smoke lit from within like clouds in an electric storm. Each corpse had been immersed in the river beforehand; the shrouds were saturated, clinging to the body so that you could make a fair guess as to the age and sex of the dead, and their wasting. Then the cloth began to dry, scorch and fall away, momentarily revealing the flesh. Friends and family milled between the pyres, chatting:

'They were related, you know. Quite close cousins, I believe.'

'He was always a good friend to my father.'

'Nice people, the whole family.'

Attendants walked amongst the fires beating down the wood and charred remains and sending up the sparks. Round the sides of the platform, the dead queued patiently on their wooden stretchers, while below the ghat, the Brahmins did brisk a trade in immersions. A cow, shambling down the street, stopped for a look and edged its way onto the ghat unconcerned by the flames. The sun began to set, the sky looking dark and the river unfriendly. Mourners peered over the edge, wondering if the Ganges would flood tonight or tomorrow night. I thought of my own grandmother's cremation (piped music and the muted hum of electric motors, and sherry), and didn't at first notice that Georgia was talking to a Frenchman she knew from Kathmandu. He had a plan.

We went to the water's edge and got into a boat that he'd hired. In the darkness, the river looked anything but welcoming, no other boatmen in sight – but our man only became angry when we suggested that the current was too strong. He would get us there, but not by rowing. He edged the boat from building to building, grabbing at mooring rings and posts, boats and ropes, cursing and gasping for breath, at last getting out and standing on the almost continuous ghat steps to pull, push and heave us. We sat silent and embarrassed by the stupidity of the whole exercise; we should have just paid him off and walked to the restaurant – called The Restaurant. There we met Mr Sanjay Rahman. We ordered lemon tea and plentiful cheap curry, and regarded him warily.

He was a very plausible young man. He'd been everywhere and done it all. He told us, without once relaxing his smile, of all the lifestyles he had tried and the amazing herbs he'd smoked in his little pipe with its curly copper stem. He fingered a copy of *Asia on $2 a Day* and asked us to update the Kathmandu section as he'd be returning there any day. He gestured around The Restaurant.

'This is where the radical politicians meet. All these people are talking politics. But it is dangerous, so they just pretend to be drinking tea.'

He got up, and said it was time to be going to the house of Pandit Shanta Prasad, where we'd be given a music recital. We climbed aboard two rickshaws and trundled through the power cut and the rain, further and further out into narrow broken streets that had me bashing my jaw on the side of the rickshaw as I strained to see where we were being taken. With every minute, I was more suspicious of the gloom and the unknown, the hiding places, the high windowless walls. I thought of garrottes, of *thuggee*, of headless corpses in the squalid alleys of Victorian cities. Georgia was very quiet. We stopped at the unlit door of a sombre house in a muddy passageway, and Sanjay Rahman jumped across the muck to knock.

There, in a large and sparsely furnished room, we sat for an hour or more listening to a serious, corpulent and extraordinary percussionist.

He hardly spoke as we entered. When Sanjay introduced us, he nodded briefly and called through an open door for his son, a boy of perhaps eighteen, who smiled and shook hands, sat obediently by his father and began playing a sitar, music lovely in itself but now no more than a backdrop for his father's virtuosity. The old man's fingers went pattering and skimming off the tabla skins, stroking them, caressing them, pressing to raise pitch, shifting his seat as he became more involved. I was aware of others watching, of family and servants peering round doorways, peeping through curtains. The son, even as he played his sitar, always watched his father. The music ended; we sat immobile for several moments, until Shanta Prasad relaxed and summoned tea.

And so – complete strangers fetched in off the street – we came away. The following morning, his son took me to a sitar shop. I still have the sitar that I bought there, though today I have had to fetch it down from the attic, and have run the shower over it to shift the dust. The original strings are intact, but feel rusty. The original wire fingerpick is still tucked onto the top bridge. It is not a grand sitar but a student instrument, made from a single gourd with a four foot neck. Georgia was unimpressed with the sound I produced from it, saying (with some justice):

'It sounds like a spider being sick.'

I nursed it around India, and ever since then I have collected musical instruments from distant countries. I have a room hung with wooden trumpets and flutes, harps and lutes, zithers and viols from Asia, Africa and the Americas – but this was the first.

In the Benares shop there were sitars and tamburas hanging from floor to ceiling, and an old man sitting in the entrance stringing a surbahar. Pinned to the wall behind him was an affectionate note:

> Dear Surendra,
>
> How I miss your shop now that I'm back in cold, gloomy London. Thank you for all you taught me, and the hours of pleasure I found in your company.
>
> Yours cordially,
>
> Lucy Irwin (Kew)

Sanjay Rahman had determined that he would be our friend and educator. It was not clear why, but perhaps – apart from native kindness, or nothing much else to do – we were vicarious travel for him; currency restrictions made it difficult for Indians to go abroad just then. He said he was the Benares agent of an 'Overland to India' company based in Paris, but was only busy from October to March. His father, he said, was a university professor. Sanjay took it upon himself to show us the town, leading us to temples and curiosities and, when Georgia started sketching, protecting her from the nosey and the offended.

'Take no notice, this man has no reason,' he announced. 'He just wishes to be a nuisance.'

He declared to me one day:

'Lord Curzon. I'm going to call you Lord Curzon. You have a voice just like Lord Curzon.'

Georgia asked him why the bathing ghats were so much smaller than they looked in photographs.

'You cannot be Lady Curzon if you are so stupid.'

'Sanjay!'

'Come on, now – you've seen the rain? The river's full up.'

He led me to a *paan* seller, declaring that it was time I learned to chew in the Indian manner. The *paan* seller mixed the ingredients to Sanjay's specification.

'Always lime and betel, you see? Now, you want gold leaf? You can have gold leaf too. It will make you very good with Lady Curzon.'

He gave me a broad wink. Georgia flushed and said nothing, and we avoided each other's eye. Sanjay returned with us to Green Lodge, where our two beds were a tousled mess of sweaty sheets, side by side.

When, later, he left us to rest, the hotel proprietor watched Sanjay walk out of the hotel courtyard.

'Do not become close with that young man,' he said.

I stared at him.

'How do you mean?'

But the proprietor would say no more, and went into his own rooms.

Sanjay seemed to know all the politicians who gathered in the guise of tea drinkers in The Restaurant. But he poured scorn on them all. We watched one man come to the telephone that was near our table, make a call and ring off.

'You see this?' murmured Sanjay. 'He's a city councillor. OK, he was speaking Hindi, so I'll tell you what he said: he was calling the Chief of Police and asking to have a particular man released from jail. He said he would consider it a personal favour. You can just imagine, can't you?'

One of the Radicals approached and informed us that a mass demonstration against the government was planned for 10 p.m. that evening. It was my chance to observe the politics of the street.

'I shall come and watch,' I said.

'Stupid,' said Sanjay. 'There will be trouble. It's too hot.'

'I'm not going to march.'

'Well, I will see you tomorrow if you have not had your skull cracked by some policeman's cane.'

The police were already gathering on the street corner opposite. Some carried rifles. At 9.30 p.m. I sat waiting, sipping my lemon tea, then pottered up and down the street attracting a few glances from the police. There was a marked lack of tension. At the nearby ghat the beggars were laid out in rows fast asleep, exhausted by the heat. At 10 p.m. a raucous band began to play: a well-dented tuba, a trumpet or two, something that my diary describes as 'an anti-clarinet', and numerous drums. Thirty torch-bearers appeared, men and boys, and were hustled into a double column.

Two demagogues began to bellow in the darkness, turning to their supporters to whip up shouts of *Gandhi! Gandhi!* A youth bore aloft a tired-looking national flag; another had a little model of a spinning wheel perched on top of a pole. A venerable Brahmin let off an immense firecracker, and they were away, screeching and squawking down the road towards the GPO with the two demagogues whipping their followers to a frenzy. The police, who had half raised their rifles when the firecracker exploded, shuffled their feet impatiently until their commander gave the order to follow. I thought it all perfectly good humoured – until I recalled students rioting over a cup of tea and being shot. So I turned into Green Lodge.

We were on a bus which was crawling through a mass of people and rickshaws. There was even more noise than usual, angry shouts and jeers rising steadily in pitch and volume. We were passing a cinema. People – men and boys only – were queuing in a solid line, squatting arse to crotch as though about to dance a low-level conga. Others displaying less patience had laid siege to the box office, shaking and rattling the bars in fury.

'Ticket touts, you see,' said Sanjay. 'It's a new film, and everyone wants to see it. The touts have bought all the R3 tickets and are now selling them for R6.'

A number of policemen, sweating freely, lost their tempers and started screaming at the mob. They began using their canes, swinging these high overhead and bringing them down hard. It was the first time I'd witnessed a cinema queue being clubbed by the police. I wondered if it would get into the papers.

To Sarnath, another of the navels of the Buddhist world: a gloomy and irreligious place, I thought. Here the Buddha preached his first sermon sitting under another Bo tree, and some of his cremated remains were enclosed in a grim heap of masonry and brick which is still there, though now the worse for wear and with little of its decorative stonework left although that little was pretty. The nearby temple was filled with poor murals by a Japanese. Only the Jain temple had signs of life, with paintings in every style from Aztec frieze to Puvis de Chavannes. On all sides were commemorative inscriptions honouring colonial bigwigs who, in the reign of King George V, Emperor of India, had donated rupees – a Buddhist revival under the aegis of the British Crown. Sanjay said there were now only half a million Buddhists in India. At Sarnath I felt their absence.

Sanjay, however, was in his element, the complete guide. He collected several other tourists under his wing and led them off. It was a picnic spot, with a deer park and concrete facilities in washed-out, once-primary colours, with Coke and ice cream for sale. Coldest of all was the Chinese temple, a tin-roofed yellow assembly hall:

This temple was erected by
Mr Lee Choa Seng
Fukien, China
1936

I wondered if Mr Lee ever saw what he'd paid for. Both Georgia and I felt cold and depressed. We drank some tea and then looked for transport home. The rain found us first, and we steamed gently.

By chance, there was a friend of Sanjay's on the bus; he offered me a cigarette without expecting chatter in return. He put me at ease, and I regarded him gratefully. He was distinguished-looking, late middle-aged with white hair, and his name was Dasgupta.

'He's a palmist,' said Sanjay, and for a moment Dasgupta scowled.

He invited us to his house for dinner, so we got off the bus and into rickshaws which took us to a miniature palace, there to recline on divans amongst silken bolsters.

He'd been a professional palmist for twenty-six years, and he began to talk like a consultant, a professional, speaking quickly with hard eyes and a forceful manner. His claims were wide ranging.

'I can even tell you the names of the girls you have slept with.'

If so, I did not want Georgia to hear it. Sanjay mentioned that a friend of his had been killed when a motorcycle caught fire; if only there could have been some warning of the danger.

'What was his name? Ah, yes – then he must have been born on February 9th.'

'Why so?' I asked, flustered.

'Is that your birthday? Then let me give you some good advice. Never join any army. Keep away from explosives, or from things that burn. Never carry a gun, especially not in your pocket. I warn you: you must be prepared to face a serious wound in your lower body – a bullet, an explosion. Let me see your hand.'

He twisted and pulled at my palm, stretching and compressing the skin.

'You have a fine moon line. You are greatly imaginative, very interested in painting, classical art, classical music, and painted dolls. You have great willpower. You never waste money or fritter it away on things that will be of no use to you. You see, your logic line is much heavier than that of impetuosity. Your thumb is rigid; you are very stubborn. Someone who loved you very much died when you were ten years old.'

What age are most children when their grandparents die? And why painted dolls? I've never given a painted doll a second look.

'Your mother has painful hands (*true enough*), and your father has high blood pressure and a red face (*untrue*). Let me feel the back of your head. Hmm, now you feel; you have an abnormal lump there. That is cancer, a tumour. Not malignant, but you should have something done about it.'

I cannot remember whether his hand had reached the back of my head before he spoke. There is a slight protuberance there but it is the occipital bone, the lower tip of my skull. Dasgupta offered to 'cure' this for me within two years by means of a certain stone, price 25 rupees, money back if lump persists. I said I'd think about it.

He turned to Georgia, stretching and compressing her hand, peering at it, and making her out as sickly and analytical by nature.

'You ought to be a doctor,' he said.

Then he offered her a full analysis at cost price, the cost being the photographic enlargements he proposed to make of her hand – a mere 120 rupees. Georgia failed badly in her attempt not to seem eager.

'I'm not sure,' she said, 'if I'd dare open the results when they came.'

'Forewarned is forearmed. I can give you peace of mind about anything.'

Georgia looked bewildered, thrilled, and worried.

Just before supper was brought in, a servant handed Sanjay a twist of paper, the contents of which he knocked back with a glass of water. There was a simple but excellent vegetarian meal served sizzling from the ghee, and afterwards Dasgupta showed me his library of textbooks, stressing repeatedly that many were written by a professor at Baroda. But he regarded me as a sceptic, and clearly did not much like me.

'You come to India in order to understand,' he said, 'but you have more laughter in you than understanding. You are not in the right frame of mind at all. There is a word that you should remember: *saama*. You will find it used often in the Mahabharata. This word indicates the manner in which you approach an opponent when you wish to negotiate – a peaceful thing, when you sincerely wish for an understanding. It is an attitude of openness which invites trust. You remember. You will learn more.'

He turned back to Georgia before I could reply.

On the bus home, Sanjay was stoned. He repeatedly apologised for taking us to see a man who had upset us so much. The bus passed the cinema again. It was 9.30 p.m., ten hours since we'd left for Sarnath. The queue and the police were still there, but quiet, regarding each other with weary hostility. Perhaps it was the second showing.

It prompted Sanjay to produce a bitchy film magazine he'd bought, and he read out the scandal about the star whose fans we had seen clubbed:

> Our friends tell us that he's arriving dead drunk on the studio sets these days. We say he's burnt out!

'It's all just a game,' said Sanjay, 'they're all trying to look daring and permissive. Film producers like to provoke the censors; into every film they put one scene to make the censors angry. But it's not a true picture of our society. We are a truly conservative people.'

He became maudlin.

'My grandfather thought he'd fix my wedding for me. He showed me photographs of twenty girls and demanded that I chose, but I refused without meeting the chick. My grandfather died soon after that, so I've escaped. My father doesn't seem to care very much.'

In Green Lodge, Georgia brooded on whether she should go back for analysis.

'What do you think?' she asked.

'You don't want to know what I think. You think my mind is closed on such things.'

'Never mind that. What do you think?'

'I wouldn't go back. He flatters, then he frightens. He's a con.'

'You would think that. I'll decide tomorrow.'

But she was not well, was eating little and swallowing pills. She spent the evening humming and drawing pictures of elephants. As we sat together, sounds of music came from the street, and a torchlight wedding procession passed Green Lodge, complete with a richly caparisoned elephant and a bridal litter, a tiny black box with prison grilles.

A quiet day pottering about Benares Hindu University, investigating an art course for Georgia, a sitar course for me, but without conviction. In the university temple – a pretty place of marble and pinkwash with fountains quivering in the garden – Georgia sat like a sphinx upon the marble with her hood concealing her face, soaking up the cool and admiring improbable statues of rhinos with waterjets spouting from their horns.

But in the evening the wind rose, the lights failed, the heat swelled and a storm threatened, and when we hurried for a last look at the riverside ghats, all tranquility fled. I had eaten something bad; I had a fluttering stomach and a pounding head and I felt in myself a flood of barely suppressed viciousness. I wanted to whip little boys who got in my way, to strangle dogs and scream abuse at any rickshaw driver who wouldn't go where and when I said. I began to understand riots; I could have used one this evening.

The Ganges was rising, swollen with bile. Rows of men sat on the steps watching it. A lizard attached Georgia. And then a Brahmin let rip, accompanied by erratic bursts of fire from small boys on monkey drums, gongs, bells and cymbals. I began to enjoy the barely incipient hysteria, but Georgia was looking worried. The Brahmin began strewing flowers on the water and lighting little floating candles of supplication which were then

whisked away by the flood and promptly swamped. Then he passed a tray of more candles among the watchers, who graced it with a few *paise* each, passing their hands through the flames and smearing the heat over their hair, just as the sky broke open.

Time to go. Sanjay took us to the station, and then vanished, walking from us as casually as when he'd bought us our first cup of lemon tea, leaving us to eat a subdued supper. The station throbbed with heat and people, the crowd interspersed with tourists carrying sitars. An unmistakeable American, off to see his guru in Baroda, accosted us:

'Hi there, fellow travellers! How's it going?'

He'd bought a harmonium.

'Hell, you all got sitars, but who can play them? Now, with this baby we can have music.'

He had no reservation, so he slept on the floor beneath my wooden shelf while I wrote with his pen and nursed my sitar cocooned in my sleeping bag, keeping a wary eye on the fleas. In the unreserved carriage next door there were people sleeping in the luggage rack.

Georgia, on the shelf above mine, poked her head over the edge and asked if I'd ever wondered how I came to be in India with her. I grinned and said I'd meant to go to America but the plan had gone wrong and she'd got me on the rebound, a mistake from beginning to end.

SIX

THE CURZONS & THE VILLAGE COUNCIL

> Once was the time… the modest maid might walk wherever she pleased alone, free from the attacks of lewd lascivious importuners.
>
> *Don Quixote*

At Kanpur station, 3 a.m., I could not sleep for fleas. I got off the train and bought a cup of tea tasting of pepper, peering about in the unreal light and faintly heady for lack of sleep. As I stood sipping, a powerfully built Sikh approached and addressed me in a rich, urgent voice.

'The tea is good, is it not? I have smuggled tea of this variety. May I ask, in all confidence, are you smuggling anything? I am by profession a smuggler. I have a farm also, in the Punjab, but my real activity is smuggling. Little things…'

He held up a thumb and forefinger: drugs, perhaps?

'I have associates in many countries, all over Europe also. I don't know why I continue; I don't need the money any more. I have a big house, I have an expensive car, and everything that I need. Smuggling is in my blood, you see; I cannot stop myself. It is hard work, my smuggling activity. I plan and plan and spend many sleepless nights. I started the hard way, with a gang in Calcutta; I was often starving. But I have studied too, with the money I have made, and I have a great many skills; you would be surprised. I can drive anything from a mule to a helicopter. You see, my business is so profitable; each trip makes me many *lakhs* of rupees. But now, listen to me: I never exploit the poor man.'

I had little choice in the listening. He loomed over me, peering very directly into my eyes.

'The risks are great, but I concentrate my will upon God, He looks after me, and I am at peace. I take no drugs, I need no women, I am unmarried. You know the laser beam? It is nothing but a concentration of light, and yet it can cut through steel. Just so, by concentrating your will, anything that you desire can be yours.'

140

A man came along the platform selling hot milk. The Sikh – who looked and smelled rich – bought us both a clay cup of milk and sat down with me in the train as it pulled out of Kanpur.

'You must become one of us,' he told me, 'and all this can be yours also. I shall give you a mantra.'

'I'm not a religious person,' I demurred.

The train rattled along through the night, Georgia fast asleep on her wooden shelf. We stopped briefly at a small station, long enough for beggars to start tapping at the window. The Sikh sat opposite me and asked where we were going, and I told him: Agra.

'Of course, you are going to see the Taj Mahal. Listen, you must learn from it, learn more of its history than that love story fit for children. Learn about the cruelty of Shah Jahan, learn about the thousands of poor people forced to build for him with whips on their backs and nothing in their stomachs. I go to Agra often but never, *never* do I go to the Taj Mahal. Your English writer Aldous Huxley called it the ugliest building in the world. So, go and see it, but know that what you are seeing is only a glittering surface about a core of blackness. And then, learn this: you too; you are a very handsome young man, you are so charming. But inside, your heart is black, as black and as rotten as this Taj, this glittering evil thing, and you are not at peace. Take this mantra! You will remember what I say.'

He stood up, and said that he would now sleep better.

In the morning we reached Tundla, where both we and the cheerful American with the harmonium would change trains for Agra. The Sikh and the American met.

'You do not look well,' said the Sikh.

'Well, no, I've an infection on my foot.'

'I can cure you.'

'No kidding?'

'Tell him how,' the Sikh said to me.

But I replied: 'This man already has a guru. He's on his way to meet him in Baroda.'

And the Sikh and the American discovered that they had studied with the same man. But the Sikh now seemed uneasy, especially when the American broke into a sacred chant taught him by the Baroda guru. The

Sikh said that the guru was now a very old man. The American thought about that a moment.

'Well, not so old. He's about forty five.'

'His willpower keeps him young,' the Sikh smiled at me.

The train screeched at us. The Sikh placed a forefinger on both our foreheads in blessing, and climbed on board.

You can take a tour bus from Delhi – 128 miles heading south – and visit the Taj Mahal, the fort at Agra, and the ruins of Fatephur Sikri all in one day, then back to bed in Delhi. Fodor's Guide said of the Taj that it was worth visiting India just for this one building. The architect Clough Williams-Ellis (a friend of my parents) once said that it wasn't worth crossing the road; Huxley and my Sikh agreed. How could I, with my rotting black heart, look the thing in the face dispassionately?

On the marble surrounds of the Taj, I tried sitting down to write my immediate impressions, while Georgia went off air altogether, hunched in a cool corner. I tried lying flat, peering up at the sky along the lines of the fluting in the white marble. I tried turning my back on the building, and gazing out over the river instead. There was a whole row of French tourists doing the same, legs dangling over the edge, backs to the tomb, a Gauloise on every lip. It had rained during the day and our feet slithered about in pools on the warm stone. We kept to opposite sides of the fountains to avoid having to speak.

The young men began to close in.

For Georgia:

'You come and have tea with me. Then we go for a ride on my scooter!'

And for me:

'Good evening, sir, what is your country? May we have friendship? I am eager to know your opinion of my country.'

There would then be a hard luck story about the difficulties of taking currency out of the country.

'And so, sir, what I am proposing is that you sign all your travellers cheques over to me and I give you any currency you like plus 7% commission. But you sign your cheques over to me.'

Among travellers, tales of such deals were legion: of counting out the money, of the rolls of dollars deftly switched so that what you thought was a bundle of twenties turned out later to be only $1 notes. I asked:

'And what will you do with the travellers cheques?'

'That is no matter for you, please, you just sign minimum $500.'

'I only have $70.'

'But I need $500!'

As Georgia tried to move about, the young men clung to her like a ploughed field to a wellington boot. We fled through the dusk. At the enticingly named Uttar Pradesh State Government Tourist Bungalow, there was milk and rosewater before supper. An amiable young man came to our table and instructed us in the art of obtaining money by prayer, so we went to bed after requesting R32,000 in used notes to be under the mattress by morning. No one had told us that the water would be turned off at 9 p.m. There was a clean sheet on a new foam mattress. To keep the mosquitoes at bay, we lifted the sheet and slept on the mattress cover with the sheet over us, side by side, not touching, sniffing at each other's sticky skin and hair.

The amiable young man had discoursed upon his God and his belief in wholehearted commitments:

'There must be no half-love or half-hate.'

He had then remarked on the love between myself and my wife Georgia, who had reddened and said nothing. Earlier that day, as we were setting out for the Taj Mahal, the manager of the State Government Tourist Bungalow had remarked on the sacrilege of visiting such a magical place 'without the loved one,' to which Georgia had responded with a sarcastic, 'Ha, ha, ha.'

Georgia kept a diary too. We scribbled obsessively, grabbing spare moments and corners of cafe tables or grubby mattresses to note down something about place, person – or each other. She asked one day if she might see what I'd written; I suggested recklessly that, once we were back in Britain, she could read the whole thing, if the deal was reciprocal.

However, the contents would not be a complete surprise to either of us by then. In Agra next morning I succumbed to temptation, taking a rapid keek at her notebook while she was in the shower; I strongly suspected that curiosity had got the better of her too. Sometimes she would announce a principle that might have kept her from temptation; she had not allowed herself to visit the International Library of Buddhism in Kathmandu because, 'One shouldn't look at books in the middle of an experience.' Such scruples might have kept her out of my diary, but I thought probably not.

And now I saw the extent to which we habitually misunderstood each other. At the Taj Mahal we had once crossed paths by the fountains; I was thinking of the Sikh on the train, of appearances and deception. I had asked:

'Have you noticed that the squares of marble are not what they purport to be, but are much larger blocks with incised grooves?'

She had recorded this, commenting:

> That frightens me, that he can be apparently so immune to the more superhuman atmosphere of the place to treat it in that cold, analytical way. It makes me inwardly accuse him of egotism and lack of imagination. That may be unfair.

Reading this with one ear sharpened for the stopping of the shower, I fumed a little – though I was hardly in a position to complain. And then I saw the following:

> Something is brewing between Jo and me, something to do with our constant physical proximity, the shared beds... It's by far the longest I've ever spent at such close quarters with anyone.

The shower stopped. I closed the notebook.

The bus to Fatephur Sikri growled across the flatlands until we saw a rock and a dark red wall half-hidden by vegetation. The ruins came into view, a long plateau topped with absurd fantasy castles in flaky sandstone, with spindly columns and low-pitched roofs between the trees.

Georgia, not in the best humour, sat down upon a wall and said:

'I'm not moving until you find the Archaeology Bungalow.'

We were on top of the hill. I was directed through one deserted palace after another to the rest-house of the Archaeological Survey of India, a large bungalow built by my former incarnation, Lord Curzon, but looking not unlike the rest of the deserted 16ᵗʰ century city: long, low arcades in red masonry. It was a sober palace for passing historians but there were none in residence, and we could have it for such a pea-penny rent that I was quite embarrassed.

The room to which I fetched Georgia had a sofa – nowhere else in all Asia had we had a sofa – and three armchairs, a writing table and dresser, wardrobe, fireplace, bathroom, thick carpeting on the floor. We felt completely out of place; we had nothing to put in the cupboards, not an evening gown between us. Our few clothes were limp, frayed and faded after weeks of being scorched, scoured, and beaten to death on bathroom floors. Georgia could not even walk properly because her shoes were coming apart. We were lowering the tone. Georgia sat upon the steps, which Lady Curzon would never have done.

But, apart from a resident caretaker and a Conservation Assistant, we had it to ourselves, with a bevy of servants to fuss about us. We reclined, we took tea, we strolled the grounds and lolled on the lawns talking with the caretaker, an anxious invalid who stayed here for the calm.

'There are times when I could wish myself away in Kashmir. For weeks we get no one, nothing, just peace – but then they are all coming. Just last week I had a terrible time. We had a very big man from your country, Foreign Minister maybe, coming to see the ruins, and we had to have tea for him. We were working so hard and I had to go to Agra to see the manager and buy so many things. And then this big man was in a hurry and he could not stay for tea.'

We dined in splendour by candlelight, Lord and Lady Curzon at a table with space for thirty, just resisting the temptation to face each other from distant ends of the French polish. Silent-footed servants brought platters of vegetable curries and tea and (greatest novelty of all) a glass jug full of water.

In the morning we took the less than baronial step of visiting the kitchen where a toothless ex-army cook taught us to make our own chapatis.

Peacocks screeched in the grounds, the caretaker sat on the lawn reading the *Times of India* and eating tranquillisers, and we gazed past him at the endless level plains broken only by some distant local storm.

In the ghost city of Fatephur Sikri – built on Emperor Akbar's orders c.1570, abandoned in 1585, and empty ever since – almost everything is built of that same red sandstone which, when wet, gives off a strange smell that at first I thought was drains or urine, but is subtler, musky, more animal. An animal scent given off by stone. In the late afternoon we were virtually alone. Everywhere the thoughts that occurred to me were stubbornly contrary. By the broad pool that cooled the emperor's private apartments, and where musicians once played from a little square island to soothe his troubles, there I could think only of the malarial mosquitoes that must have bred in the water. In the Hall of Private Audience, where Akbar sat atop a massive sandstone pillar reached across four bridges and carved with eclectic imagery of wisdom, I could only think of a spaceship. Under the main gateway, the stonework showed traces of the paintwork that was once everywhere in the palace – so I found myself thinking of Viollet le Duc discovering that the façade of Notre Dame in Paris had once been painted and gilded, and recalling how the British Museum had scrubbed the last vestiges of colour off the Elgin marbles. The Fatephur Sikri paintings had weathered down to soft pastels, a mix of flowers and abstract patterning having a spurious air of innocence.

All around the empty city on its rock, the interminable flat countryside spread, the same in every direction. It was unsettling to look at; I thought perhaps Akbar couldn't stand it, and so had left.

Hymn singers at Fatephur Sikri.

In the entire deserted city there were perhaps half a dozen people. I sat in a corner of the mosque arcades humming to myself. An unusual echoing sound began, accompanied by a rippling and pattering that ran under the vaults. Two musicians with drum and harmonium had sat down in the centre of the open mosque facing the tomb of Sahikh Salim; they were singing hymns to the saint, and the notes were blurring in the multiple echo under the arcade. They wanted money off me. I brushed past them into the tomb.

Nine colours of stone were used there, the light diffused through screens of drilled marble lace-work, a design of flowers and stars tempting destruction with the hubris of its delicacy, like the colours swirling over a soap bubble that you cannot help but touch. For all the delicacy of the work, the sheets of marble were quite thick, and the inner surfaces of the cut-out shapes were reflective. The red stone buildings outside appeared as a blurred silhouette that wavered as I moved about, as though seen through imperfect glass.

The saint slept in a dark, richly decorated inner room, in a tomb of reeking sandalwood set with mother-of-pearl. Georgia said she wanted it as a bedroom, then blushed at her own impiety.

At evening in the bungalow, by candlelight, Georgia objected to my writing so much. She said that she needed one full page for each developed idea, which is as much as the well-groomed brain should attempt to hold at any one time. She said that I had mental cystitis, squeezing out little droplets of unrelated thought.

Georgia was pottering on her own through the Hall of Private Audience when she was trapped in a corner by a man who closed in upon her under the red pillar. She screamed her head off and he vanished, leaving her to emerge a moment later into the puzzled presence of a large group of Japanese down from Delhi for the day.

Thereafter we went about together. The tourist buses were all gone by four p.m. We sat on a turret, trying to imagine the sandstone palaces full of carpets. I watched the evening while Georgia sketched the architecture, and we had the place to ourselves once again.

Until a man in a loud red shirt waved to us from a distance. He climbed up to our tower, accompanied by a young friend who said that he too had studied this architecture, because he was a carver of miniature mosques and Taj Mahals for the tourist trade. Redshirt dwelt at length on his ambitions in the film industry, of his power and influence in the village that huddled at the foot of the rock, and (heatedly) of his envy of young Europeans able to travel where they liked. I watched the sun setting, and Georgia continued to draw turrets.

It was 5.45 p.m. We had ordered dinner for 7 p.m., and decided that first we would walk down the hill and have a look round the village. Redshirt and his friend came too. The young carver led us to his house and offered us butter.

'Butter? Why does he think we want butter?'

'I'm not sure. Wouldn't you like some butter?'

'Butter! Butter!'

The boy gave a sweet smile and presented us each with a glass of water. He then led us to a small courtyard where a circle of gentlemen drew up chairs for us and introduced themselves as the Village Council. The Assistant Overseer of Works invited us to eat with him.

'My speciality chicken – famous! I cook him myself. An experience not to be missed in India.'

It was now 6.30. Our dinner would soon be waiting for us at the Archaeological Bungalow.

'All ready, though!' said the Assistant Overseer. 'Just a taste before you dine.'

We moved to an inner yard where there was a small tin table that wobbled on the bricks. The Overseer shouted for some glasses, and produced a bottle filled with a brilliant yellow liquid. Redshirt laughed aloud.

'Now then, this man says he is a follower of Mahatma Gandhi, and he is wearing shoes made from cows which have died by themselves, but here he is giving you whisky which the Mahatma cursed.'

The Assistant Overseer sniggered:

'Ah, but so good before my chicken.'

Large tumblers were placed on the table and filled with the yellow whisky topped up with a very little lemonade. The Assistant Overseer said:

'Elephant Brand whisky. Made from bananas.'

It tasted strong, not unpleasant. He refilled my glass to the brim. The Assistant Overseer had already swallowed two tumblers, and his eyes quickly went bleary. He sent out a small relative for more, while Redshirt murmured to me:

'This man cannot live without whisky.'

A new bottle arrived, pink this time. Georgia's glass was replenished. The Assistant Overseer was by now a happy man, his voice thick and slow:

'I... am the flame... of the divine. I am the flame of the divine! Yeeeessss. Every man too, there is no doubt, the flame of the divine.'

Georgia – at her most charmingly giggly – showed him how to drink a friend's health with interlocked arms, to his great delight.

They all misconstrued her name.

'Health, Madame Gorgeous! To your most wonderful health.'

I vaguely registered that a third bottle had arrived, now crimson, tasting stronger yet and more medicinal. Where, I wondered, was the chicken? The Assistant Overseer was swaying on his chair, filled with the fire of the divine. I tried to pass on to Georgia, as elliptically as I could, Redshirt's information that the man was an alcoholic. I could only manage:

'Georgia, sweety, this guy's a lush.'

Redshirt pounced.

'What is this word, please? What is lush?'

I was about to explain that the Assistant Overseer was a man of great originality of spirit, when Georgia spluttered:

'A lush is a ponced up dandy.'

The rest of the Village Council stood in a circle about us, smiling benignly, as Georgia promised Redshirt that she'd come back and be his leading lady in the movies. At well past seven a woman called from an upstairs doorway that dinner was ready. We teetered up precipitous stone steps and sat on a rush mat with a plate of chapatis and a pressure cooker full of ferocious chicken curry. Hungry and merry, we wolfed the lot, bubbling incoherently about palmistry.

It occurred to me that it was late, and very dark. We stood up – and Georgia at once looked extremely drunk. I felt quite steady and leapt down the stairs with great agility, only to miss the last step completely and land in a heap in the dark courtyard. Georgia was carried down. A torch was produced. With myself and an amiable Post Office clerk supporting Georgia, we attempted to move very slowly up through the steep, pitch black lanes, Georgia swinging her legs in any direction but forward, as we wobbled from side to side off the track into the long grass, talking all the way. I was trying to reassure her.

'OK, good, good, you're fine.'

'Don't you talk good good pidgin to me. I'm not fine, Oh, so many hands, get off me, stop groping!'

Three sober and respectful local government officers came up from behind and took her in charge.

'All is well, Madame Gorgeous, you are now with us.'

Not once did they drop her, though she thrashed and wobbled and attempted to roll back down the hill. We lurched through the dank animal-reeking palaces. Georgia began to panic, and to fight off the arms that supported her.

'Stop groping! Please! Oh my God!'

'Madame, please do not be worried. I think that this is the first time of tasting Indian whisky. We are with you now.'

They were the soul of honour. At the Bungalow steps they let Georgia gently to the ground, swearing that wherever she went they would provide an escort. We crawled – literally – into our darkened room.

A candle appeared at the door.

'Do you want your vegetarian dinner, sir, for 7 p.m.?'

I had no idea what time it was, but felt shamed and obliged to make amends.

'Of course.'

I wobbled alone into the dining room, and sat with three candles and three silent servants at the head of the polished table with food enough for a royal family, all stone cold. I made myself eat, while the servants watched, expressionless. I attempted to sit upright, to look like Lord Curzon, and to talk calmly and clearly. I failed, blundered back to our bedroom and collapsed in the toilet, staying there till dawn.

In spite of the water having failed – which had perhaps once led to the abandonment of Fatephur Sikri – we elected to stay. We would give ourselves an extra day to recover, chewing pensively on boiled eggs and parathas at 11 a.m. Reading *Don Quixote* on the lawn did not work: too many flies. We remained in the cool of our room, reading and writing and arguing about poetry until, at 4 p.m., we went again into the deserted city. Georgia sketched, while I lay on the warm slabs and watched the colours of the sandstone and marble changing as the sun declined. Piles of baroque cumulus, inhabited by cherubs with hangovers, boiled in the afternoon heat.

One of the palace guides – Rajo, who had been witness to the débâcle of the night before – spotted us on our tower and climbed up, to talk about Akbar and Aurangzeb, Jahangir the Drunkard, and the poems in

Farsi painted on the walls of Akbar's bedroom, the 'Dream House'.

'I too am a poet,' he said. 'I have been a guide here for twenty-two years to feed my family, but I am a poet. I will tell you two lines of a song that I have written.'

'A song? Won't you sing it?'

He shrugged, hesitated, then sang a few lines of Urdu, very softly, with the same moaning cadence that the hymn singers had used before the mosque.

'That's lovely,' said Georgia, and he blushed.

He told us of 'Poet Functions' at which one hundred poets declaimed in all the languages of India, often accompanied by a harmonium. He himself had recited in public at the Red Fort in Delhi, and now he would type out some verse for me. He led us off to see some of the embarrassingly large number of buildings that we had been too idle to explore, invited us to lunch the next day, then apologised for leaving us, saying he must be home early tonight, because he had got to bed very late. He had found the Assistant Overseer lying in the road, and had been obliged to carry the poor man home and put him to bed because his wife would have nothing to do with him.

A fine evening of vivid skies. For a long while, Georgia and I did not speak; I watched her work on her light-hearted, almost frivolous sketches. At last we walked home and ate a supper of curried eggs by candlelight, and were regarded by the staff as imbeciles for continuing to do so when the power returned. We had begun to feel new trust, to understand that we would care for each other. There was a cricket somewhere in the room, and we'd been promised caramel custard for breakfast. Georgia washed my sun hat. Life was good.

Mid-morning, Rajo re-appeared, dressed beautifully in perfect white. He had not done the translation of his song.

'Ah, I am sorry, it was very difficult. But I have brought you an invitation from the Water Engineer.'

I remembered a cool, thin face in the shadows of the Assistant Overseer's courtyard. The Engineer had been one of our escort home. He had been blessed with a son one month before, and today there was a thanksgiving feast.

Everyone was on best behaviour; the Assistant Overseer was so smartly turned out as to be barely recognisable. The Water Engineer had had three daughters and had begun to despair. Many men, said Rajo, would have blamed their wives, but the Engineer was educated and generous. He had prayed and prayed, had paid a Brahmin a great deal of money – and now there was a son.

He and his wife were in the courtyard, sitting on a mat in front of a small brazier and tossing spices onto the coals while the Brahmin chanted. There was a portable shrine with a tiny brass Ganesha, and a great deal of flowers and finery. Redshirt and friends looked indescribably pious, while the Engineer and his wife were quite overcome by joy and were struggling not to grin unbecomingly. Suddenly everyone got to their feet; while the Brahmin chanted louder and louder, a young boy hammered at a gong with such ferocity that Redshirt motioned him to calm down. They all began to murmur blessings: may he shun Elephant Whisky; may he not die in pain. The candle was passed round; we dropped a few *paise* onto the tray and smeared the heat over our hair. Small dishes of ceremonial food were blessed, and a little of each tossed onto the fire. Then each person was handed a piece of paper with a spoonful of squash and sweet semolina, onto which was dolloped a little curd. That was the ceremony.

An hour later, crowds of people arrived, and we were feasted in three shifts. Twenty guests at a time sat in a bare room upon mats on the cement floor. Women and girls bustled in and set before us platters of palm leaf pinned together with twigs, with a clay cup and two small clay dishes. They returned with brightly coloured plastic buckets out of which they shovelled curries, *kachuri, purri,* sweetmeats, a curious sweetened wheat flour and a thin curd drink, all in an endless supply that never let one empty the plate. Stuffed gentlemen leaned back against the concrete walls and belched contentedly, surveying the chaos of leaf-plates, curries and coloured buckets. Then we rose and made way for the next shift. Rajo whispered to Georgia that, as the only lady at the feast, she should go and thank the women of the household, which she did with good grace.

And that was the celebrations done. The earlier ceremony had been intimate; the banquet was public and impersonal. But the happiness of the Water Engineer and his wife was everywhere.

We parted from Rajo, Redshirt and the Village Council. They had all taken a shine to Georgia:

'Good journey, Madame Gorgeous.'

'You will return and be my leading lady!'

Rajo pressed a bundle of *beedis* into my hand for the road. The Engineer asked my age, and refused to believe that I was just twenty. I took off my clean sun hat and gave him the most youthful grin I could manage.

'No, not the hat; the face is older.'

I had aged.

The want of linen, and scarcity of shoes, thinness and baldness of their clothes, and their surfeiting when good fortune throws a feast in their way: this is the difficult and uncouth path they tread, often stumbling and falling, yet rising again and pushing on.

Don Quixote

SEVEN

THE WORLD UNDER THE TREES

> He could not believe that so curious a history could lie for ever
> inevitably buried in oblivion. And therefore he would not give
> over enquiring after the continuation, till at last he found it, as the
> next book will inform the reader.
>
> *Don Quixote*

We were waiting for a bus at a tiny village called Krowli at 5 p.m.,
wondering where we would sleep that night. Standing out in the street, we
were conspicuous, and the air was heavy and electric with a threatening
storm. A myopic middle-aged man approached, inviting us to sit in his
shop which he indicated nearby, and to have a drink while we waited.

The walls were lined with bottles. I said under my breath:

'What do you think this is? A chemist's?'

'Rubbish, it's a whisky shop.'

It was a doctor's surgery, the examination room open to the street with
a stone slab covered with a mat for a couch. A stethoscope was the only
visible equipment. In exchange for a tune on my recorder, the physician
served us fresh lemonade. The thunder rolled. As the bus crossed out of
Uttar Pradesh into the supposedly arid state of Rajasthan, a deluge of such
ferocity began that passengers opened umbrellas inside, there being no
glass in the windows.

At Bharatpur, some thirty miles west of Agra, we came down a peg.

The dak bungalow – lodging for government officials on tour, or for
foreign waifs and strays – had formerly been officer's quarters in an army
camp. The room was vaulted and had French windows, but the ceiling
sagged and dripped and the paint was hanging off the walls, while the air
shrilled with mosquitoes. The bathroom was so thick with wildlife that we
didn't even consider it for a pee. I could imagine Somerset Maugham
characters blowing their brains out here, and had the feeling that, if I
tweaked at the rotting plasterboard, I'd find a stash of gin. There was no

food; the power failed, and the shifty little caretaker wanted me to pay for a candle. Outside, the rains drummed down; we took off our clothes and stood under the cascades coming from a broken gutter. Later a single 25-watt bulb started to glow. We jammed a towel under the bathroom door to keep the insects at bay, festooned the room with dripping shirts and underwear, sat at separate tables scribbling to keep hysteria at bay while longing for gin and daylight, then pulled our bedsheets over our heads. There came sepulchral bugle calls in the night, heard through the storm.

At 6 a.m., without breakfast, we set off walking to the Keolado Ghana Bird Sanctuary.

It was much further than I had expected; I began to feel light-headed. We came to the Rest House, took a back trail, and the landscape changed entirely, opening out on either side of the path into a vast marshy lake swarming with bird-life: fish-eagles and kingfishers, scores of spoonbills and herons, egrets and ibises, cranes and painted storks.

We wandered along the dykes between water, reed and tree, giddy from amazement, sleeplessness and hunger. An owl stared down at us, frogs plopped, cranes clattered, and there was no sign of anyone. We sat for the best part of an hour on a stone bench, staring at trees out on the marsh which creaked under a weight of cranes and storks, and wishing we could get closer. Then Georgia muttered:

'Oh fuck – humans.'

Three smartly dressed gentlemen came down the path, talking volubly. I asked politely if I could join them and hear a little about the birds – and so I learned of resident species and migratory species from Siberia and Kashmir, their feeding, mating and nesting habits, why the shallow lake was ideal for them – and why we should go and collect our bags and move in directly. This was the warden; he had received my letter, of course he had.

But first we should join them in a boating expedition. With water almost over the gunwales, we punted over the marsh and crept in beneath the nests, until storks spread their wings over our heads.

At R20 a night, even with food included, the rest house would soon be beyond our budget, but it was fabulous while it lasted, and gave us a great luxury and novelty: two sheets apiece. They brought us breakfast of toast and tea, left us to sleep, then called us to lunch: mutton curry, fruit and a light custard pudding. We were very happy. The two early morning bird-watchers – vets from Jaipur – drove us into town to collect our bags and to have Georgia's plastic flip-flop mended with a replacement strap. I booked us back into the awful dak bungalow for tomorrow night, grimly amused at staying on the premises of Public Works Inspectorates, and wondering if in Cambridge you could request a bed in the Rates Office.

I sat on the verandah gazing out at the greenery, and reading a little. I now alternated the misadventures of *Don Quixote* with chapters of Thomas Mann's *Magic Mountain*:

Hans Castorp gathered a bunch of all this loveliness and took it back into his room…

A tall, well-groomed, white-haired Indian gentleman came out of his room, smiled at me and then moved about the verandah. Suddenly he exclaimed:

'Good heavens – Gonville & Caius!'

I looked up, startled.

'Please forgive me: I was glancing at the register and noticed your entry. Now, I climbed over the wall, the Senate House Passage wall of Caius in… when would it have been… 1937, I think.'

A Cambridge-educated lawyer at the top of his profession, Government Advocate to one of the larger States of India, and now rather jaded by jurisprudence.

'I do sometimes wonder: was it all worth it? I believed that I would be working on behalf of people, of humanity indeed, but really in India it is a struggle to perceive the humanity behind the writs. You British left us a fine legal system but in my heart I believe that it never could have been successfully adapted to the Indian situation. You see, British law is at base a law for individuals in opposition or conflict. But in India we are dealing with masses in conflict. We do not murder the individual for his money if there is any possibility of a group of us getting together to murder an entire village for its land.'

He was there for a short break with his girlfriend; the warden called her Mrs Vinata and treated her with great deference, because she was – apart from being a consultant surgeon in Delhi – a bird fanatic, a regular visitor of sixteen years' standing, who lectured us on the best times to see each bird.

So, at 5.30 that afternoon, we set off again with the boatman who punted us over the marsh. He was in love with every creature.

'Yes, please,' he purred happily, 'this bird, and this painted-er stork.'

As the sun went down, the squadrons returned, and the trees swayed under the crush of painted storks, lovely ivory egrets, and the ibis with a snout like an anteater. Cranes the size of ostriches waded close by. Water buffalo looked at us long and hard, convincing Georgia that they meant to charge, but they tossed their horns contemptuously and wandered off. A group of deer with Landseer antlers let us get close, then one of them gave a tremendous bark and Georgia all but fell in the water, spluttering:

'Is it fair to disturb them?'

The sun faded tastefully into the mist with mother-of-pearl colouring, and the pretty jakanas, their white wings trimmed in black and with a long feathery tail, fluttered in to land like butterflies. The egrets had the expensive elegance of a gift from Harrods. All the colours, except for the aniline brilliance of the storks' beaks, were soft.

At supper – a meat curry followed by jelly and custard – we were joined by the lawyer and his lady, who appeared dressed as if for a banquet, deliciously scented. Mrs Vinata could think of little but the birds.

'It's another world out under the trees.'

The advocate gazed at her adoringly. A gentle, autumnal romance.

> I thought thy frequent visiting of the bottle would make thee fonder of sleep than of music.
> *Don Quixote*

With our light off, longing for sleep but waiting for a bearer to bring us some drinking water, there came a knock at the door: not the bearer, but a small man with large, round spectacles.

160

'Please forgive me for disturbing you, but may I ask if you like Indian folk music? We are having a programme upstairs; would you join us?'

In a large reception room, some two dozen respectable persons had gathered for gay home-grown amusement. A group on the floor had a harmonium, fiddle, drums and bells. The little man with spectacles tied bells about his ankles and began to sing to the accompaniment of the harmonium and tabla, dancing slowly as he sang, every so often leaping high or stamping his feet to sound the bells, or dancing like a snake. Then he sat and began some simple, merry songs from a book while the drummer pulled at one belled leg and a lady in a sari pulled at the other.

Everyone was drinking, either a spiced cold tea or gin. Someone was attempting to record the songs on a poor little machine but there was too much talk. To begin with, the singer concentrated, but soon the gin did its work and they began to lark about, pulling each other forcibly up to dance and fighting in play. The bottles emptied steadily. Georgia was cornered for conversation by a woman in a rich green sari and with an attractive face from which the youth was beginning to fade, called Aruna.

A huge, jolly gent arrived to cries of:

'Ho! Traffic jam!'

I was called upon to perform, fetched my recorder and played some cheerful Telemann.

'Aha!' cried Aruna, 'you are a musician. Now you shall play the harmonium and sing to us.'

'I've never played a harmonium, I'm afraid.'

'But of course, anyone can play – any real musician.'

The harmonium was the little sort that requires one hand to squeeze the bellows while the other fingers the keys. Dull despair came over me. I sat on the floor, trying to think of the simplest tune that I could pick out. What came into my head was certainly the most inappropriate song ever sung at a party in India, a ghastly dirge about the Irish potato famines:

Oh the praties they grow small over here, over here,

Oh the praties they grow small,

And we dig them in the fall,

And we eat them skins and all, over here.

'Ah,' sighed Aruna loudly, 'he sings like Krishna.'

Krishna bewailing the 1846 Sligo potato crop was too much. The harmonium and I wheezed to a stop.

The party was becoming raucous. Aruna was very interested in men. She tugged at Georgia's sleeve, pointed to a burly but good-looking fellow who was pinning the singer to the floor in a playful half-nelson, and simpered excitedly:

'He's a bachelor!'

The bachelor gave me another gin and murmured that Aruna and the old harmonium player were members of what had once been a ruling Rajput family:

'Really there is no place for these people now. They have some land but they will not go into business. They have some influence but no power. So this is how they pass the time.'

Aruna pulled me up to dance, with much waving of arms and twisting of wrists. It was time for bed. The power failed and the heat was stifling, but nothing could stop the revelry upstairs. Just before I fell asleep there came a terrifying crash: Traffic Jam had had an accident.

Mrs Vinata was in a very ill humour at breakfast. The party had slithered into a drunken riot, only ending when the warden had forcibly expelled them. He apologised profusely when Mrs Vinata protested that this was a bird sanctuary, not a third-class hotel in the bazaar.

But she and her gentleman-lawyer had been out at dawn for a last boat trip under the acacias.

'It's another world beneath the trees,' she said again.

They left us their addresses in Delhi, and departed.

As the morning heat built up, we sat glumly counting our cash. Time and money had become disjointed. In weeks of travel from Istanbul to Nepal – some three thousand five hundred miles – I had spent £30. When I flew home from Bombay, £89-worth of travel would pass in fourteen hours. At the bird sanctuary we were living beyond our means, and gloomily prepared to return to the drear dak bungalow.

'What are you doing?' protested the warden. 'You cannot go; I wish you to play to me again upon the flute. I shall give you the room half price.

Also you shall tell all your friends in England to come. If I don't have more guests they will close me down.'

And for another tune he loaned us two bicycles.

We pedalled to the far end of the lake, where there was a huge concrete monument commemorating the former rajah's epic shoots, held each year from 1902–1964. They came in migratory droves: Lords Kitchener, Wavell and Harding, royals from Afghanistan, Germany and Nepal, and a certain Mr Jack Denton Strong and friends from America who slaughtered four thousand birds in one day. Nor in war was there the slightest let-up – not until the killing ground was declared a sanctuary.

'There's a horrible snake!' squeaked Georgia. A long silvery neck rose out of the water, a submerged heron on a feeding prowl sticking its snout up for air every fifteen seconds or so, like a snorkel. Near the rest house there was a baby wild boar trapped in a pit. The warden complained about the problems the boars created, and declared that someone would have to eat it.

The advocate had left us his *Times of India*. The following report received some eight column inches on an inside page:

30,000 FLOOD-HIT MOVE OUT TO SEEK FOOD

About 30,000 agricultural labourers of Guriadhap Pargana and Goalpara are on the move, seeking work and also food and shelter. They have been uprooted from their lands following waterlogging of a vast area by floodwaters.

These people, along with their families, are trekking to safer places, carrying whatever they can on their heads. Batches are fanning out towards Kamrup, Darrang and Lakhimpur districts, probably with the intention to occupy forest land if possible.

Some of these people are taking shelter at railway stations of these three districts. Many of them leave the stations to beg in surrounding villages, and then move on to new places. They are also stated to be selling their belongings to buy food and other necessities.

Thousands of dwellings have collapsed. These areas have successively been experiencing floods during the last three years.

163

Last year too, crops raised by these migrants were completely destroyed…

An eyewitness from Goalpara said that the migration reminded him of wartime. Pale and emaciated men, women and children were on the march for days together in order to reach a railhead. Most of the people had no other cloth except small pieces to cover some parts of the body…

That evening, Georgia was upset. As she wrote her diary, she was pestered by ants, and flapped at them irritably. We undressed and went to our twin beds; I lay thinking of the line of her hips and back. In the dark, she said:

'I need you to restore my sense of the ridiculous. Do a ghost impersonation.'

So I floated about the dark room with a sheet over my head and a pen torch shining, making stupid noises.

'That's enough. Please will you scratch my back so that I can sleep.'

I found my way to her bed. She was lying face down.

'You can sit on me,' she said.

I turned the sheet down and sat on her bottom, and ran my fingernails up and down her back, feeling a light debris of sebum, sweat and skin fragments collect under my fingernails. She lay very still. I thought about kissing the back of her neck, but did not.

'Thank you,' she murmured.

On the crowded train to Gwalior, I met another poet. He was a shy secondary school teacher of English, who said that he felt discouraged above all by a feeling of isolation from the mainstream of English literature.

'And so, you must tell me: should I read T.S.Eliot? I have heard that I should, but I am not so sure.'

He demanded from me a list of notable English novelists, playwrights, critics and poets that he should be reading. He sighed:

'But I am afraid that these books will be so costly.'

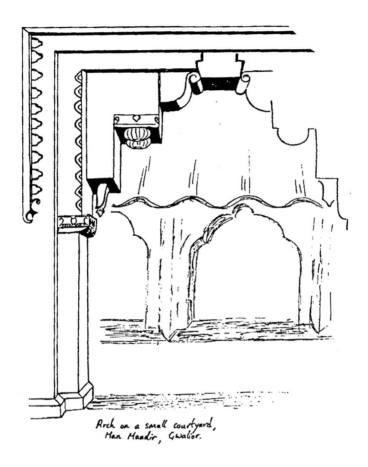
Arch on a small courtyard,
Man Mandir, Gwalior.

I said that they weren't cheap in the UK either.

'But you are, I think, a wealthy man.'

'Not at all; I'm a student. I have very little money.'

'So, your parents are wealthy.'

'I wish they were.'

'Then how is it that a poor student can come all the way to India?'

I explained that the government paid for my time at university, and that my college had given me a small travel grant.

'So, you are an envoy here on a government mission. But tell me, what report will you be taking back to your government?'

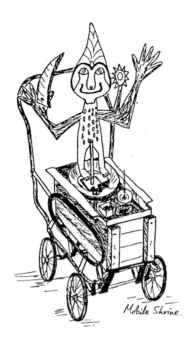

Mobile Shrine.

We walked from the station to the hotel; it was cool and only a short distance, and saved us a rupee or two. The whole length of the tree-shaded road, five rickshaws hovered about us like pilot fish, engaged in a running price war, bidding each other down to absurd sums like 25 *paise*. Later we walked the evening streets of Gwalior; half the town was heading for the cinema, and huge film posters hung on every wall. The men in these posters shared an expression of sensitive, brilliantined cretinism, whether hero, villain or buffoon. Crowds milled around the cinema gates, and policemen in pairs stood watching, twitching their long canes. Smartly dressed men arrived on bicycles with their wives perched on the luggage racks anxiously holding their saris out of the spokes. When we sat down to eat, a crowd of urchins gathered to observe us with worried expressions as though they expected us to blow up. In the street nearby was a mobile shrine mounted on the chassis of a pram, a tin sun growing from one bicep, a sickle in the other hand.

Returning to the hotel through the dark streets, with only the light of feeble yellow oil lamps in the back corners of small, cave-like shops, I imagined that I was in Kathmandu once more.

We sat at our bedroom table in the Regal Lodge and I scribbled all that I could remember, wondering in a student-ish way: 'What am I learning? It is all too much; am I taking in anything at all?' When everything, even the serving of a cup of tea, was so different, how was it possible to think clearly without familiar points of reference? I had begun to wonder if I was becoming dependent on Georgia to keep me alert. I watched her for a moment; she was packing an aerogramme with her tiny handwriting. I could see my name upside down:

Jo is quite closed to all outside influences and distractions.

I speculated who she was writing to: some mutual friend, doubtless. I intercepted and killed an ant that was making a foray from my collar towards my ear.

'Heartless beast,' she said.

'You actually think,' I retorted, 'that I have a small mechanical pump instead of a heart.'

At which, having just sealed that letter, she turned crimson. She undressed and lay down.

'Scratch my back again,' she said.

Sitting on a wall below Gwalior fort, I gazed down into the city below. Ceaseless noise reached me: not traffic, but hammerings, sawings, voices shouting, screeching, babbling and occasional laughter. The homes below the fort were clustered in yards or alleyways sometimes paved in herringbone brick looking like ragged basketwork, with tiny houses, seldom more than a lean-to shed. Around the wooden or corrugated walls, the charpoy beds leaned up on end, while others were occupied by people sleeping in public. A few cooking pots stood amid small piles of rubble or scrap metal or heaps of washing. Through the trees came wisps of smoke. Young men drifted about, seemingly aimless. I tried to imagine living down there and sustaining the drive and morale to 'raise' a family, to improve its lot. Everything was bound in predatory cycles: the people hunted scraps of cash or food; in the air directly in front of me, swifts flicked about after insects; high above, hawks and vultures swirled on the wind, watching.

Few of those children below ever got to school; it was not compulsory. But up above, within the walls of the fort, was a snobby public school. A gaggle of teenage girls passed us; they were fresh, self-confident, beautifully groomed, and greeted us in the soft, rather lovely English accents of the Indian elite, then wandered away past the Man Mandir palace that was cold, elegant but bleak. Hungry again and light-headed, we entered a small tea shop and devoured eight tiny bananas, seven samosas hot from the oil with a sharp mango sauce, and four cups of tea, for less than R4.

As we walked down the hill, at a fork in the road we met a beggar squatting on his haunches. He had a long-necked, two-stringed lute resting over one shoulder, and plucked at one string rhythmically without varying the pitch at all. In the other hand he held little finger clappers with built-in jangles. We paid him for a song. He sang cheerfully, producing a remarkably effective sound from the barest of resources.

Do you like Indian folk music? they'd said at the bird sanctuary, before getting pissed and fighting.

The door of a nearby house opened and an old man appeared, none too affluent himself. He had a lovely, civilised face. He was carrying a small saucepan out of which he spooned into the musician's bag a generous serving of food, before giving us a quick smile and bustling away indoors.

EIGHT

RAILWAY CHILDREN

Up early, at the station early, we bought tickets early and were ready for the early train from Gwalior to Delhi, scheduled to arrive after lunch. But we had misread the timetable; there was no train until half-past one, and that would not reach Delhi until mid-evening.

Georgia was in a dangerous mood, sick, tired and despondent, with red watery eyes and 'Oh, it's not worth it,' to every suggestion. I drifted up and down the platform taking an interest in the design of clock faces and the manufacturing provenance of cast-iron pillars. A tall European, young and well dressed, stood looking disconsolately at his watch.

'Morning,' I said.

'You wouldn't be going to Delhi, would you? Somehow I've got the times wrong and I'm stuck here for three hours or something dreadful.'

'I think it was last year's timetable.'

He was English, and his name was Edward. He carried a long bag of stiffened cloth, which looked empty. What had been in it?

'A fine English shotgun. I came out as delivery courier to a shotgun.'

He and Georgia played chess in the tearoom. The station was filling up and a knot of angry men had gathered at one end of the platform. I asked the tearoom bearer what they wanted.

'A big fellow from the Railway Ministry will be arriving. These are on-strike railway men and they have lost their railway homes and pensions, so they are waiting to show themselves.'

Suddenly, the angry knot began shouting and gesticulating. The Punjab Mail was coming, like a dozen beehives pulled along on a string. As the train stopped, would-be passengers mobbed it, attempting to push their luggage in through the windows but prevented from doing so by the people climbing out. One woman succeeded in thrusting a large white bundle inside only to see it jostled for a moment or two and then disgorged to flop pathetically onto the platform. Hands groped out of every opening – even through the toilet window – feeling for little clay cups of tea. Excited tea-vendors rushed up and down supplying every

170

hand, then jumped about in anxiety until the hand reappeared with money.

We stared in dismay; it seemed inconceivable that one more person could be added to the melée, let alone three plus a sitar in a sleeping bag. The tearoom bearer, an imposing man, seized my orange rucksack with its red straps and rattling swivels and marched to the train door, roaring commands. We followed helplessly. By dint of worming, scrabbling, acrobatics, brute force and – above all – the courtesy of other passengers, we found ourselves with half a seat each, a few slats of wooden bench where we remained immobile for six and a half hours.

How pitiful British train journeys seem by comparison. Would an English rush-hour crush make space for two shabby young Indians, feeding them tea and crystallised pumpkin? In India by now I felt cheated and uneasy if someone on each train didn't offer me a snack. But I never saw the big railway fellow arrive at Gwalior, nor heard what had happened to him.

That evening, at New Delhi station, we had hoped to be collected again by Dr Hari Munshi, my family contact from home. I had sent a telegram from Gwalior station, from an office full of clicking brass machinery in mahogany cabinets and men with agonised expressions pressing their ears to black horns. But it had not worked. We stood in the dark forecourt of the station, and he was not there.

I tried phoning, without success. We ate a sullen supper and phoned again, and still no answer. We sat silent and illegal in the First Class waiting room playing miserably on our skin colour but attracting increasingly mistrustful looks from the bearers. We phoned again at 10.30 p.m., and at 11.30 – at which point the waiting room closed.

'Shall we look for a hotel?'

'I'm too tired to move.'

'A Railway Retiring Room, then.' But they were full.

We took a deep breath, and joined the sleepers in the station foyer where they were numerous. We spread waterproofs and Georgia's sleeping bag on the cement floor and drew our possessions in between us and a large pillar. Surrounded by families huddled under dirty white sheets and old blankets we looked regal, all colour, red, orange, green and blue of rucksack, anorak and sleeping bag.

A policeman stepped over the bodies towards us.

'No, forgive me, sir and madam, but you cannot stay here.'

'We must, we have nowhere to go, and we're waiting for someone.'

'Please go to a Retiring Room.'

'They're all full.'

'But you cannot stay here on the floor.'

I gestured in silence to the sleepers all about us; the policeman shrugged sadly and moved away. We settled down to rest, and the station grew quiet.

And then, pandemonium. A baying pack surged into the concourse and ran towards the platform gates, howling with rage. As I opened my eyes, there were men leaping over me, kicking and tripping over the sleeping families in their fury, yelling for the blood of someone who had just got off a train.

We huddled behind the pillar until they were past and onto the platform, where the noise died down as quickly as it had started. The intended victim had not arrived; possibly he was already dead at Gwalior. A few minutes later the demonstrators left, pouring back out into the forecourt, gesticulating and punching the air in frustration. Slowly, apprehensively, we stretched out again on the cold concrete and slept, and at some point in the night the lights in the concourse went out.

The station came to life at 5 a.m. when the first trains started running. A tubby railway official stalked through the sleeping crowd, admonishing everyone:

'Get up! Please get up! This is not Calcutta, this is not Howrah!'

Why did he bother on this particular morning? The sleepers must be there every day. And why did he speak in English, which most of them would not understand? Was it our presence that disturbed him, as it had the policeman? No one moved except me; I got up, looking for a pee and a hot drink. But the tea was foul and chemical. I accused the stall-holder of putting New Tata Detergent in his brew, and I refused to pay full price. He clawed at my arm for a while, but exhaustion had made me stronger, and I had plenty of aggression to spare. The usual tout whispered at my ear:

'You want cheap hotel? Change money? Hashish?'

I spun round on him:

172

'I'll find my own fucking hotel, you creep! Curl up and die!'

I shocked him for the sheer fun of it, for the delight in throwing off restraint, to see a small man wince. It was a complete failure; the young man was tougher than me, and merely laughed in my face. I stalked off looking for a loo, and availed myself of the air-conditioned Taj Express which was preening itself on Platform One.

And so at last we left the station to find a motor rickshaw – which promptly ran over my foot. It didn't hurt in the least, but I was so tired that I burst into tears.

As part of our preparations before leaving Britain, we had fished around for contacts in India. So we had arrived with the addresses of three surgeons.

On first arrival at New Delhi, back in July, I had gone to the office of the Railway Police and asked if I could phone a doctor; a car had come to fetch us, the driver swearing that his brother was a professor of engineering in London. And so we had come to Dr Hari Munshi's private plastic surgery clinic, where we slept on steel hospital cots.

Dr Munshi loved to talk. At meals he would prattle excitedly about politics, language, cultures. I only needed to feed him a question every quarter of an hour and he would rattle on. Georgia was appalled, thinking that I applauded the conservatism, the elitism, the chauvinism. How can I know what he's like, I answered, if I don't let him talk?

On our return from Gwalior five weeks later, the clinic was busy and we could not stay. Nonetheless, they packed food into us. We were summoned to the consulting room and sat with Hari behind a little cotton screen while the table was loaded with toast and fritters. In the evening, we all went out to dinner. Hari had a daughter called Rita. I thought she might be seventeen or thereabouts; she was just thirteen, but had all the self-confidence of the expensively educated. She tried to whisper to me about boyfriends, but Hari wanted more serious talk. Rita's idea of a good evening out was not a discussion of medical ethics with regard to Untouchables, but a trip to a disco with her friends. She ate heartily, finishing her meal with a chocolate ice-cream sundae called a *Miss India*, of a glutinous sweetness to explain the girth that some misses of India reach in their twenties.

Hari tried to order Scotch and soda, but his wife wasn't having it.

'My God, no! No, you do not have a whisky! I am sick and tired of your drinking.'

Hari looked mournfully at the empty beer bottles. Then he reproached me across the tureen of cooling meatballs.

'You've not eaten your dinner.'

'I'm afraid you gave me too many fritters.'

That's what came of living hand to mouth; someone puts a plate of fritters in your way, and you don't think twice.

At Hari's clinic there was a letter waiting from Angela. She was living in luxury in an ex-High Commissioner's house in Sri Lanka, surrounded by children, cats and wonderful food – except that she had dysentery and could not eat it. The letter was addressed to me. Angela drew a verbal picture of me reclining in the lap of luxury dressed in pure Afghan whites, drinking iced gin and listening to sensual chamber music. It was a curious stab at the truth; I thought of Shanta Prasad the tabla player in Benares, and of Elephant Whisky.

Georgia did not feature in the vision at all, but got a kiss and an afterthought. She was hurt, and said:

'I don't think Angela likes me very much.'

Angela wrote:

'Being alone, even for so short a time, has taught me very surprising things about myself and my limitations. I must say this: I don't miss you.'

We headed for the new bazaar – Pahar Ganj – street after street choked with carts and signs and tiny shops and people dozing in public.

We moved into Mukhesh Guest House, and things immediately looked up. The room was a smaller version of that lovely room in Benares with the same colour scheme, a faded and flaking green gloss paint on the walls and a red tiled floor. It was small, square and a bit grubby, with garish

Hindu deities in three-colour prints, little statuettes of Ganesha painted in bright colours, and bundles of incense asking to be lit. There were two inner windows with bars to keep cats and burglars out, and a mysterious trapdoor in the floor. There was a low, rough wooden table to write at, and a large clay water pot with incised flower decoration, in which a sterilising tablet soon effervesced. We had hard but comfortable wicker charpoys and dark red striped sheets, one each as usual. The toilet and shower were down precipitous outside steps in a yard where dark corners accommodated whole families. We were one hundred yards from New Delhi station, two hundred from Connaught Place, right in the heart of the capital of India and paying 12 rupees per night. The proprietor bustled about having the room swept and fetching clean sheets and drinking water, welcoming and keen to make us feel at home. But what made the room special was the French window opening onto a balcony over the street

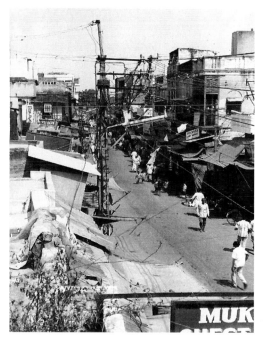

Below us was a vivid turmoil of commerce, ebullient and brightly lit until well after midnight, selling foods and leatherwork, brasswork, household plastics and padlocks, incense and enormous apples, mango milkshakes and shirts. Our street did a good line in small travel agents with promising names: Sham Travel and Subhash Voyages. There were also numbers of textile shops, and to enter Mukhesh Guest House we walked in through the proprietor's fabric emporium. One street nearby sold little but jewellery.

Of a morning, the bazaar woke slowly, yawning, rolling up its shutters, rubbing the sleep out of its eyes and the dust off the plastic pots, the ropes and detergents, bicycle tyres, mattresses and mats. First to stir were the food vendors, the teashops, sweet makers and titbit fryers who would fan energetically at their charcoal braziers and begin filling trays and bowls with the crisp and the sweet, the greasy and the savoury in heaps or neat stacks.

Barrows appeared selling luridly coloured lemon juice and freshly crushed sugar cane. Ox carts would arrive laden with produce; one morning there was a hopeless muddle outside the Guest House when two heavily laden carts, both swerving to avoid a cow, somehow got their wheels interlocked; there was a great deal of angry shouting and gesticulating from the drivers who kicked in vain at each other's spokes. Fruit and veg men came onto the street with baskets of mangoes and okra, bananas and onions, sitting in the shelter of the enormous carts.

Also early to open were the rice and spice shops, with mounds of grain in a dozen subtly different colours in tins and in sacks with their tops neatly rolled down, with pepper, paprika and pulses, turmeric and scrolls of cinnamon, and box after box of curiously scented powders. These shops would be besieged by women as soon as the shutters went up, while the men wobbled past on bicycles or retreated into teashops with a newspaper.

I wandered about snapping and sketching, buying a bunch of small bananas which oozed over the camera, obliging me to eat them as fast as I could. I took photographs with one hand and stuffed bananas into my mouth with the other, tossing the skins under barrows like everyone else but feeling painfully conspicuous. I ate the first piece of cheese I'd seen in weeks: fresh, cool, delicately pungent goat cheese displayed on wet leaves among the melons.

As the day waned, too many people attempted to walk out, to buy, to sell, to promenade, until one could scarcely move in the bazaar at all. Only the *paan* sellers benefited from the crush. Fat merchants, despairing of forcing a way through the crowds, would stop pushing and buy themselves restorative *paan*. The *paan* seller worked at high speed, cracking betel onto a leaf, smearing on lime, adding the extras to taste. Boys sat by huge bales of leaves, trimming and splashing water over them to freshen their sheen.

All this I could watch from our balcony, or from the nearby teashop. There I'd observe the proprietor concocting sweets, evaporating milk ever so slowly in a metre-wide shallow pan, stirring the sugary goo thicker and thicker, and sprinkling drops and pinches of flavourings from the perch where he squatted above the fires. Other pans held boiling oil for the jalubees. Nearby was a giant vat of curds which, for a few *paise,* he would spoon into a tin mug for me, pounded up with ice.

But we were never free of the need to plan, to negotiate. Georgia went to Baroda House, headquarters of Indian Railways, to obtain our student concessions for the journey to Bombay and Hyderabad. It was the first time she'd done such a thing on her own and of course she coped perfectly well – indeed better than I would, being less inclined to go off into rambling conversations about the joys of India's transport infrastructure. But she was not to be persuaded of her own abilities, and looked decidedly nervous as she set off.

At the Ambassador Hotel, we re-confirmed our flights home with Egypt Air, still some way off.

'To London?' cried the clerk. 'You are going there? You know about London? Ah, but I have been so worried. I have to visit my family in England next month and I shall have to take the train, and for so many nights now I have lain awake thinking, how can I find my way across London without the most terrible mess-up happening to me? Please, will you tell me how to go?'

I told him, and then worried all day that I had told him wrong.

In Connaught Place I went into a music shop and bought spare strings for my sitar, and also paid R10 for *A Simple Introduction to Indian Classical Music* by one Swami Prem Vedant in which I read:

> The 31-year-old Swami makes it clear that he is not a playboy of the Western World out to sample the pleasures of the east. The only son of a wealthy bank manager in Denmark, Swami Prem Vedant left home at the age of 18 and travelled widely...

I still have the book, but I have never read it.

We went looking for supper, and sat down in a curry shop open to the street. Along the front, a low wall contained a slow coal fire, and a man sat at a table nearby rolling out chapatis. Coal dust scrunched underfoot. In such places we ate our very best meals: dhal and breads and curried baby peppers, all for a few rupees, with glasses brimming with sweet tea. The cook had a saucepan into which he slopped milk and water, then a large spoonful of sugar and another of dust tea. The pan went on the fire and was brought to a rapid boil before being strained into a glass. It was like a nectar, smoky and very sugary. If I drank that in England I would throw up; perhaps it was to do with the heat. A thick, clammy darkness enveloped the bazaar at night.

Georgia discovered a perfume stall and began opening bottles of every scent in the Orient, jars of incense, body and hair oils, and oils to massage the muscles of dancers. There were dozens of bark and flower extracts, heavy oils without alcohol that weighed down into the pores, reeking of expense. Cavafy (my favourite poet at the time) had written of:

Sensuous perfumes of every kind;

As much as you can get of sensuous perfumes.

Georgia began to embalm me, touching my hands and arms with a haze

180

of samples: jasmine and geranium, saffron and musk, camphor, cardamom and clove, lotus and lavender, violet and vanilla, pineapple, patchouli and peppermint, lemon, anise and orange, gardenia and frangipani, lily of the valley and 'oil of the soil', eucalyptus, cinnamon, amber, zinia, night queen, narcissus and rose, orchid and sandalwood and even plain 'bouquet'. We sniffed, we smeared, we bought a few, together with essential balm for the consequent headaches. We were all nose. We hunted coarser scents to rasp out the dense vapours of the perfume stall, sidling from shop to pungent shop. Someone had set fire to a pile of fouled straw in the street and we approached it, allowing the smoke's stink to smother us. The heap of straw was large; there was a wind and the streets were narrow. A number of people regarded the blaze apprehensively. I envisaged my sitar catching fire, the dry gourd cracking and flaring as briefly as a match. At the end of the street, near the station, was a fruit stall where the fruit was not for eating but for crushing into sybaritic drinks. We had three: one of milk, apple and rosewater which left the palate as fragrant as a walled garden in a medieval allegory; another packed with mango; a third of milk and pistachio.

In the guest-house bedroom, I cut Georgia's hair with nail scissors. She still smelled of perfumed oils and smoke. I loved sitting close behind her, looking closely at her skin, lifting her hair from her shoulders, smelling it and hearing the scissors scrunch through it – just as I liked scratching her spine and rubbing her shoulders. And taking her hand to pull her across busy streets. But I would not offer any more than that, sure that I would be slapped down.

Our room was filling with objects and colours, the sitar, books and scents, half-burned joss sticks and folds of red and orange rucksack, red-gold curls shorn off Georgia, and all our trifles, diaries and half-finished letters. It felt like home, though we were only there a few nights. Alan Ginsberg in India was able to stop and wait for the changes in himself; he had six months in Calcutta and Benares. How stupid it was, trying to take in India at speed. I thought, risibly, of John Wayne leaping from his horse onto a runaway stagecoach; his horse had to be travelling at exactly the

same speed as the coach, but I could never move at the same speed as India, and was in danger of missing my jump and falling in front of the wheels.

The moon was nearly full, the street lined with empty motor-rickshaws, as neat and still in the dark as dormant snails. Everywhere there were people sleeping: on charpoys out in the street, on the ground, or on concrete ledges along the front of shops; beggars, rickshaw drivers, tradesmen and cows. An American girl had moved into Mukhesh Guest House and now occupied a charpoy on the open landing. The colony in the room opposite seemed to multiply. I washed our clothes in a bucket under the communal tap, creeping stealthily between the sleepers but dripping detergent on them. Downstairs, I glimpsed a shady room full of serious gambling faces and thick smoke, from which I heard the *flick flick* of cards and the rub of coin pushed over a wooden table.

We went back to our books. Georgia when reading threw out a string of unrelated remarks, scraps for my nutrition. She turned a page of Ginsberg's *Indian Journals*, and chirped:

'Ooh, look at this, the Patna-Benares train, oh no, we went to Gaya.'

Or she would quote a pleasing sentence at random, or a judgement thrown into the silence.

'Amazing and silly woman!' (Anna Karenina.)

Georgia asleep in
Guest House

The fan, the light and everything electric in the street expired. For a few minutes I wrote by torchlight. Then Georgia took off her clothes and lay down with her back to me. Without being asked, I sat on the side of her bed, gently running my fingertips across her skin, catching the last of those preposterous scents on her. After half an hour, the lights outside came on again, but we remained in the darkness. Apart from the slow rheumatic hum of our fan, and the distant puttering of a motor-rickshaw returning to roost, the night was silent. It did not feel in the least like the heart of a teeming capital city. Georgia rose, wrapped some cotton round her, and sat out on the balcony with her insomnia. The walls were crowned with cats, the room full of moonlight.

Saturday in Delhi. The politicians – who couldn't bear the thought that one might forget them over the weekend – started our day at 7 a.m. with a fantastic crash, rattle and slam of drums and cymbals and a dozen brass, starched white uniforms with gold braid and black peaked caps, and two men in smart dark suits riding on a cart and hectoring the still shuttered shops through loudhailers.

At 8.30 a.m. we waded against the current in streets filling with people heading for the station. Over a railway bridge, through an arch, and we were out of New Delhi and into Old Delhi where human life was, if possible, yet more concentrated, and it brought out the best in Georgia who nosed and trilled and chattered with pleasure. The architecture became Victorian Tropical with wrought-iron façades dripping people and saris hung out to dry in the dusty sunlight. The walls were coated with a flaking yellow wash, while every external fitting, every column or door frame or lamp was daubed in old greys and greens. The streets served as factory, bedroom, market, nursery and playground, teashop, impromptu law court and public forum, where cars were a thorough nuisance and were given a butt in passing by the moral cows.

Two-wheeled bullock carts had great cross-bars at the front for harness, behind which the snooty-faced beast put his shoulder hump and shoved, very slowly. If the cart stopped, the bar was swung up into the air out of the way, like a wooden arch. When the carts were parked in long lines with all these bars raised, a sort of pergola was created. The horns of the oxen became entangled with the bars as impatient young men yoked them in with a lot of cross clattering, and small children stood staring at the enormous animals, until a toss of the horns sent them scurrying for safety.

Around the walls of Shah Jahan's mosque was a barrier of stalls and carts, tea kettles and curry-on-the-spot men, bicycle repairers, welders and mattress stuffers and stitchers. The approach to the mosque was littered with scraps of kapok and horsehair, rusted spokes and slivers of rubber. For 75 *paise* we could climb the mosque menaar on condition (said the sign) that we did not smoke or sing lewd songs. The claustrophobic staircase had the familiar urinous odour of Indian sandstone, but from the top the muezzin had a wonderful view, though he was unlikely to be heard. We looked down on the backs of hawks and pigeons circling on the breeze with sun on their wings. Every two minutes an automatic bird scarer detonated, and the flocks burst clattering off the rooftops as though the domes fizzed. The birds streamed in a tight circuit of the courtyard, some of them failing to allow sufficient velocity for the return landing and being whipped back into the open by the wind.

Far below, I viewed with startling clarity the boys stuffing and stitching new mattresses, some of them half buried in kapok. I saw a motorcycle skid to a halt, its panniers entangled in a passing pony trap which dragged it backwards along the ground ten yards or more.

Half the city was visible, as far as the New Cantonment. The Fort was very near – but I could not take another fort. To the north was the golden dome of the Sikh temple. There were the two railway stations, old and new, and Parliament House in the distance. Every structure was patched, adapted and extended, the roofscape an impossible hatching of tiled slopes with little apparent relation to the tenements below, the logic further blurred by tangles of phone lines and illegally-tapped power cables. In two rooftop cages, groups of schoolchildren were doing their exercises, the girls groping after their own thrashing plaits. I began to think of drains, imagining the city with all the solum removed so that every underground pipe and wire was exposed, a fantastical mesh.

I took a detour down narrow lanes where every inlet between the buildings was an outdoor room for a family, and where ladders led to the rooftops, cooler for sleeping. It being the weekend, the children were all at home, sitting about on charpoys or playing with their baby sisters. The children swarmed over everything, half-joking, half-hostile. Many had spinning tops which they sent into a spin with quick whippings. An urchin ran out from a passageway and thumped a well-inked date-stamp onto the front of my shirt, disappearing back down the alley while everyone slapped their knees and guffawed.

The lanes were full of industry, making and selling: food and shoes, leatherwork, woodwork and tin, small-lathing and small-printing, and shops in caves and cupboards or half-hidden behind exquisite façades. I saw a particularly fine old doorway, a deep arch elaborately moulded and painted with two tall flanking niches and a crude awning overhead. I took my time preparing to photograph it, waving a light meter hopefully, taking a first trial snap, then realising I was being eyed by three young men.

Suddenly one of them closed on me with an aggressive monosyllabic demand:

'Why?'

'Oh. Why not? Do you mind?'

'Yes, I mind, I mind very much, everybody here minds. You go and you photo the Taj Mahal and you photo the Red Fort and you don't come back here, you don't come in here and photo these bad places so that we must be ashamed. You get out now. You just get out!'

Two or three others were now ranged behind him; clearly they were not going to let me have a decent sight of the door. I was only there out of admiration.

I fled back to Georgia.

Delhi was too much; there was more than I could comprehend. As we walked I found my concentration failing, so that at last I could hardly see what was in front of my eyes – like trying to read when over-tired and unable to focus. I vaguely registered a traffic jam, and that I needed food, and that on the bridge over the railway there were stalls cooking lentils for the tonga drivers, while a solitary woman sat under a tatty umbrella failing to sell a bunch of fast blackening bananas. And finally I wept a little, though without (I think) Georgia noticing.

The water in Mukhesh Guest House had failed, and the amiable proprietor sent the smaller members of his family scurrying next door with buckets on our behalf, while the adults hammered and cursed at the pipes, trying to shift the airlock or blockage.

What greater joy, after a morning in Old Delhi, than to sit with a bucket on the cold stone floor of a dark shower room sluicing icy water over neck and groin. I sat in my underpants in the sun doing the washing, while Georgia slumped for the afternoon. I sat on my bed looking at her, while listening to the ebb and flow of sound rising from the street.

Breakfast in Delhi.

We were sitting in a favourite tea-shop consuming slices of white bread and sweet tea from scratched tumblers, and we both began to draw as representative a vista as we were capable of: in Georgia's case, this was the whole street; in mine, a tiny scene of a water urn and jars.

For once my lack of ambition paid off; Georgia soon had so many inquisitive people standing in front of her that her drawing was aborted. They then watched in awe as she wrote another aerogramme.

Out of the crowd, a man spoke to me in confident English with a surprising American accent. He was aged thirty-something and was dapper in a blue shirt and white kipper tie.

'Good, it always pleases me to see artists here in India, where life itself is an art.'

'Goodness,' I blinked. 'Is it?'

'As is friendship. Friendship is a special art.'

'That's very true.'

'Personally, I would say that you English have a much greater capacity for friendship than you have for love. That is what we Indians have found.'

'Perhaps you're right. You have an unusually American accent for an Indian, if you'll forgive my saying so.'

'My mother is American, and right now I'm working at the American library, so. My name is David.'

He sat down, and grilled me for half-an hour on the art of travelling as a poor student, as though simultaneously fascinated and repelled by the notion. I couldn't imagine David doing anything of the sort.

'What would you say was the most important asset for friends travelling together?' he asked. 'Practicality, or mutual loyalty?'

'They may be the same thing.'

'Indeed. Do you like photographs?'

He would not be denied. He led us both to a small photo studio a few doors away, failed to persuade me to put on a tie but succeeded in brushing my hair, arranged three chairs and posed with us for a portrait. Then he paid the 7 rupees, left his address with the photographer, took down our names and addresses in a manner which suggested that he had no intention of forwarding prints as promised, and said:

'It's for my collection, you see.'

I remembered Gellir and John in Herat, with their gallery of passport photos of 'all our friends.' David shook everyone's hand, and vanished. We never heard from him again.

I asked the photographer:

'Are those photos black-and-white or colour?'

'If you would like them colour, we can make them colour. It will take two days only.'

There was a young man sitting at a table in the corner with an anglepoise lamp, a jar of brushes and a row of small bottles. With infinite care he was tinting a wedding portrait. The effect was ghoulish.

'They'll be fine as they are,' I said.

Back in Mukhesh Guest House, we were relaxing in our room reading and writing when one of the proprietor's sons came in on a social call as they often did. Georgia happened to be sorting bits of paper from her

wallet; these included a small photograph of Sanjay from Benares.

The boy picked up the photo and stared at it.

'I know this man.'

'I don't think so,' said Georgia. 'He doesn't live in Delhi. He's a friend of ours in Benares.'

'I don't know his name, but he is a very bad man. He stays here two month ago. Very bad! He run away without pay. He owe 200 rupees.'

'I don't think…'

'Yes, wait here, please!'

The boy ran off downstairs and returned with the hotel register. He flicked through the pages – and there was Sanjay's name and address.

'Well, why haven't you done anything about it? You could find him very easily.'

'Yes, but we cannot.'

He would not elaborate. I remembered the manager of Green Lodge warning me against Sanjay. But he had been a friend.

We took a bus to the Munshi Plastic Surgery Clinic for dinner, and arrived in the middle of frenetic activity with patients, parents, children and servants all flustered. The daughter Rita wanted to gossip, but was made to go to bed early with the other children and was very peeved. She handed me another letter from Angela.

We had brought Hari Munshi a bottle of KAT 29 whisky from Kathmandu, but he had finished it all the night before and was in disgrace.

'Even when we were courting he compromised me,' said his wife. 'He would go and play golf and then he would get himself completely drunk. So then we would go to the cinema together and he would fall asleep and snore and snore until I became so embarrassed that I had to take him home. Is that the right thing for a nice Indian girl?'

She recounted her own medical career as a model of how not to promote the interests of nice Indian girls. Her father had decided when she was still *in utero* that he wanted his child to be a doctor. When she came out a girl, he threw family and caste objections to the wind and made a doctor of her. Some of the family had never forgiven him.

'You British,' said Hari, 'are always denying your traditional prejudices and insisting on your freedom of action, while in reality no race is more hidebound. We Indians are always proclaiming our traditions and claiming that they govern our every move, but in reality we obey them only when it suits.'

Dinner was magnificent: beef nestling in spinach, curried chicken and mutton, half a dozen vegetables, and a *raita* with miniature crisp pakoras swimming in the sour, spiced curds. Then pistachio ice-cream, a large block of it; Hari and I devoured three-quarters between us.

'And now,' said Mrs Munshi, 'we shall have dessert.'

Out of the kitchen came the boy bearing a dish of chocolate custard. I regarded this much as a distended Strasbourg goose views a field of corn.

But Mrs Munshi studied it with deep suspicion.

'It has no crisp top. It should have a crisp top.'

The kitchen boy said nothing.

'What has gone wrong? How much sugar did you put in this custard?'

Still the boy said nothing, but gave me a nervous grin. Mrs Munshi plunged her little finger into the custard and tasted it.

'No sugar at all, my God! You have put *no sugar* in this chocolate custard – are you an idiot now? Here, you take this away and we shall all just starve here.'

Back in the guest-house, I took out Angela's letter, cross with her for addressing it exclusively to me. There was nothing in it that Georgia should not have read, and again she was hurt. We sat in private patches of moonlight half the night, not speaking, listening to a patrolling policeman with a heavy *lathi* cane tapping his way up and down the bazaar. Cats gathered on the walls, and the fan went dead.

We had gone out in too much of a hurry last night; although I had put my padlock on the door, I'd neglected to put the chain on behind the lock, so the door was not fastened. The manager, seeing this, had put on his own small padlock.

When he opened it for us, I looked in apprehensively, half expecting to see a vacant space where my camera should be. Everything appeared to be there – except my knife.

One should not get too excited about a knife, except that it was a rather fine Norwegian knife with a blackwood handle and a blade of laminated stainless steel and carbon. It had been expensive, and I would claim insurance if I could report its theft to the police and obtain a document. Oh, but really, I thought, I can't bother the police with the theft of a knife, can I? On the other hand, it might be a chance to talk with a policeman.

In the Central Police Station, armed constables directed me through a large courtyard to an untidy office. The duty sergeant called for tea.

'I am sorry,' he said, 'that you have come here to complain.'

'Oh. Yes, I'm sorry too. It's just a small theft. A Norwegian knife. Nothing important, I know, but it was good quality.'

'Of course it was, or you would not be here complaining. But you see, everything that you people bring to India is costly.'

'I'm sorry.'

'I'm sorry too. You will never learn, and you will be robbed again and again. We Indians take nothing with us when we travel – nothing but our clean linen.'

He sighed a sorrowful sigh and gave me a page torn out of an exercise book on which to write my report.

'Where are you staying?'

'In Pahar Ganj.'

'Of course, but which hotel?'

'Mukhesh Guest House.'

'I guessed it, I was right! Don't tell me – the front room with the balcony?'

'How did you know that?'

'Because that is where all you people stay. We have so much trouble there. Trouble with women. A dirty place.'

Very deflated, I walked out through a yard now crowded with lorries into which riot policemen with canes and shields were clambering. I turned for refuge into an art gallery. Among the pseudo-ethnic clutter there were some lovely paintings in hot colours, and a modern wood carving of a

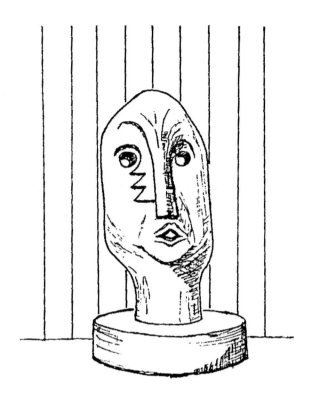

head around which three rich English ladies milled enthusiastically, determined not to buy without haggling.

The gallery owner was not interested in haggling. He came and spoke to me simply to get away from the ladies. I said that I liked the paintings.

'Yes, they are good, don't you think. They are all about heat, because India is all about heat. But Europeans do not take account of climate when they buy paintings. Sometimes I have letters from people who have bought a painting from me and taken it to Paris or Munich or London and they ask if they can send it back because they don't like the colours any more. I always say to them: think of this in your London winter! They don't listen to me. I like to sell to Japanese, who have more sense.'

In Connaught Place the heat was thrown at me off the filthy flanks of airline buses. The tonga horses stank of sweat and stale. A row of women squatted roasting sweetcorn; passers-by would stop and crouch only to take a light off the coals for a cigarette. A man sat on the pavement winding a pair of snakes about his wrists, one grey, one pink.

At last we left Mukhesh Guest House, heading for Bombay. The only transport big enough to carry both of us, with our rucksacks and my sitar in its sleeping bag, was a splendid iron and mahogany carriage towed behind a motorcycle, a thunderous vintage BSA single that fired barely twice a second. But nothing can thunder through Delhi; the streets were choked with bullock carts full of baskets of chickens, and handcarts full of charcoal, vegetables, beds and cooking pots. Loose cows ambled against the stream of traffic. There were thousands of bicycles, millions of people. The old BSA farted and protested that it wished to show its paces on the open highway, and that it considered such wriggling and creeping between bullock carts beneath its dignity. It stopped. The driver kicked; it spluttered, and died again. A cow rubbed the headlight with her snout, nudging us backwards. The driver kicked and kicked the motor – then got off and began to shove us and his contraption through the crowd.

'This is ludicrous. Shall we get off and find something that goes?'

'No hurry. Anyway, I can see the station, over there past the cabbages.'

The engine fired again, and the driver grinned and jumped on, laughing like crazy at the joke and relieved not to be seen pushing his machine into the station forecourt. A great joy came over me, a delight in the absurdity and all the amiable chaos and the cows through which one pushed a taxi. I grinned like an idiot.

'Here!' cried Sancho. 'Here are the bulls, and I am an earl!'
Don Quixote

198

NINE

BOMBAY BEAUTY BAR

The Paschim Express waited fluting softly through its brake pipes; we sat in the buffet eating eggs on toast regarding the train warily, as though it might go off unannounced, or perhaps get lost, wandering off across the Deccan plateau to dump us in Madras. On the platform, two ascetics stalked up and down leering at everyone through beards and rags, giving an occasional hop, skip and jump of pleasure.

We had bought dharis, thick cotton mats in bold coloured stripes, which is what the cognoscenti sleep on in Indian trains, and we spread these on our reserved shelves. We shared a bay with a small child and its parents; the father bullied wife and son equally, and pigged himself on rice and pieces of chicken. I put myself to bed with a banana and a clay cup of tea, and thought about what was coming. We would re-meet Angela in Bombay, and it seemed an oddly retrograde thing. The caring affection that had developed between Georgia and me might be set back to what it had been in… where? Tehran?

Half the night there was a hard, fluorescent moonlight that turned the trees black against a livid earth. For mile after mile there were stretches of water beside the track, populated by reflections of palm trees. But the waters had receded: no clouds, no puddles. At dawn we crossed a broad, dry river bed. The land looked parched and sorry for itself, gouged by a thousand cartwheel ruts which there was neither wind nor rain to smooth, only the next cart.

South of Baroda we clattered across a river so broad that I momentarily imagined I was crossing the Amazon. It was the Narmada River, about to debouch into the Gulf of Cambay. I peered hopefully past the head of the bullying father who was asleep with his chin on his chest, and wondered if I could see salt water. At Bombay I would have my first sight of the ocean in months, and my first ever meeting with the Arabian Sea. I thought of these things because I knew I smelled dreadful.

As I watched the landscape, it began to change. It became tropical and brilliant; the soft greens switched to emerald, the palm trees grew steadily bigger and a line of high hills came into view inland, sharp and angular rock masses draped with vegetation like thick green sponge. The bully woke, and informed me that we were now passing through the tiny principality of Nagar Haveli. The Paschim Express would pause enquiringly at small stations and the platform hawkers would have something new to offer at each stop. There were green coconuts which they would decapitate on the spot, while huge green plantains nestled in the same baskets as tiny milk bananas. There were fruits that I had never seen before; one looked like an overgrown passion fruit – a mangosteen. Another was light brown and the size and shape of a plum, fibrous but ingratiatingly succulent inside with hard black pips and an erotic, perfumed savour somewhere between medlars and rosewater. The juice was strange, thin and watery but with a way of setting into an astringent tack in the back of the mouth. A sapodilla.

And at last, the sea. We rolled past Santacruz airport, from which we would soon fly home. Georgia shuddered:

'Looking at my own grave.'

We had a second contact here, another plastic surgeon. We stood, apprehensive, in the foyer of Bombay Central, hoping for Dr Uttara.

'Do we telephone?'

'We have to try, I suppose.'

But nothing came of it. These medical contacts were mine, and Georgia held me responsible.

'Now what are you going to do?'

'I'll take a rickshaw.'

'There aren't any rickshaws in Bombay, only taxis. You'd know that if you'd read Fodor.'

'Then I'll take a fucking taxi.'

Yes, the most important assets for friends travelling: practicality and loyalty. I left Georgia eating more eggs in the station. In Delhi, all taxis were Ambassadors. In Bombay they were, without exception, Fiats. Travellers hang onto such scraps.

I went to the Sir J.J.Hospital. I searched, I asked, I rode up in a steel lift cage and passed on the third floor a frightening asylum of silent staring people behind a decorative ironwork screen. But no one knew anything, not even the porters who, as I begged them to recall one of their own surgeons, shrugged their shoulders. Until a man in paint-spattered overalls, with excellent English and an impish smile, leaned over the counter beside me.

'Who are you looking for?'

'Dr Uttara. The porters have never heard of her.'

'Of course not; they have never heard of anybody. I, however, am a sign painter, and I know her well. Very nice.'

He reached over the head porter's desk, rifled among his papers and produced a staff directory which told me all about her.

'But before you call her, we two shall have a drink together.'

At a stall in the forecourt he bought two bottles of *Limea*.

'If you wish to know anything in an Indian hospital, always go to the painters. These porters run about, they try very hard to look busy, they are very proud, but they never stop to talk to anybody. The sign painter must be still to do his work, so he talks to people, people talk to him. He knows everybody. And so I say, good day to you, sir, and I hope your operation is a success.'

At dusk we drove right around the bay, along the pearl-strung waterfront of Marine Drive and past the apartment blocks high over the water, at last finding ourselves in luxury on the second floor. The rooms were huge, cool and sparsely furnished, with a number of good paintings. Silent servants removed our bags, sitting us down in oversized armchairs by an enormous orange television. Washed and fed with apples and cold beer, I subsided into the cushions and looked gratefully at Dr Uttara.

How old could she be? She looked no more than twenty-five; her letter had been written in a babyish little hand, and she was given to giggles and wriggles. She was pretty, with puppy fat and sparkling eyes and something Iberian in her looks, a hint of Bombay Portuguese. She chattered about her job and said that some of the paintings were hers – bright, smiley things in Expressionist colours. I was entranced, my pent-up affections wanting release.

She was a paying guest here; the owners, Major and Mrs Singh, were retired, and exuded wealth. Mrs snapped her fingers to conjure a meal concluding with rum truffles. Major Singh scrutinised me, concluded that I was starving and gave orders through the kitchen hatch – which to my embarrassment resulted in a plate of scrambled eggs. The lovely Dr Uttara asked sweetly what sleeping arrangements we would like, there being only one spare room, with a double bed.

'Oh, that's fine,' said Georgia quickly. 'We've been sleeping together for months now, like brother and sister.'

Perhaps not quite what she meant.

I woke early, wrapped myself in a towel and a Tibetan jacket, and sat surveying a view like some tropical Naples: pantiled rooftops, small windows with wooden shutters, and mottled walls. I looked at Georgia dozing; there was a lock of hair lying over her cheek. I wanted to reach out and tuck it out of the way, but her own sleepy hand did it.

At breakfast, the genial major sat surrounded by toast and eggshells, energetically pounding aerogrammes with a rubber stamp.

'All for Flushing.'

He saw me watching him.

'These are for my boy Praveen, who is studying in Flushing, USA. I write to him every day to exhort him, and so I have a rubber stamp for the address. I buy these aerogrammes one hundred at a time.'

In the Victorian canyons of Bombay, splendid signs swung above the street. On a giant dangling padlock was painted:

WELCOME AT GARUDA'S

HOME FOR LOCKSMITHS!

Nearby was the reassuring:

IMPERIAL EMPORIUM

FOR EVERYTHING

There were traffic-jammed windings, broad avenues of plate-glassed boutiques, and as many traffic lights as taxis. Victoria Terminus put St Pancras to shame, with grand staircases spiralling up corner turrets, delicate tints in the brickwork, and terracotta-coloured blinds flapping at the open arcading at every level. All around stood dinosaurs of Colonial

Gothic, covered in swirling carved detail so elaborate as to prevent one focussing on anything.

At the GPO *poste restante* there was a telegram from Angela with her time of arrival in Bombay, and a letter from my cousin in Cambridge:

> It's odd to write to an address like *poste restante*. The words seem to connote a limbo. Envelopes resting, messages of hope and grief poised, uncollected. To write to such a place demands a particular irrelevance.
>
> I visualise you finding it (if you find it) with American elbows fastened firmly into your ribs on each side: 'Will you take a look at this? They've filed half the letters under first names. I'm going to have to search till doomsday to find that check.' The chins bob and tuck over the variously coloured envelopes. For some the home that was abandoned just weeks ago now stands for all that is clean and sane in the world. A member of each group guards the rucksacks in the corner, the canvas blues and reds bleached and sand-rubbed. The remnants of national emblems hang by hasty stitches which fastened the particular optimism of being German, or British or Swedish to so many things that would have been better left behind. Whatever your emblem, beside a dust road at dawn you must squat to excrete like any peasant, make your ablutions and leave before your smells sigh back at you.

I might have envisaged a fellowship of old acquaintance at the *poste restante*. But the travellers of summer had long dispersed. The steady stream pouring through the sanctuaries – the Pudding Shop, Amir Kabir, Sigis, the various Green lodgings – we had lost them, had debouched into India and sunk like silt. A German standing nearby claimed his letters, but we did not know him.

There was one other letter: from Angela, addressed to Georgia. Having read it, she passed it to me; it was distinctly half-hearted. Tomorrow we would meet her again, and would have to re-accommodate her. Who would now sleep beside whom? Who would cut Georgia's hair, or scratch her back as she fell asleep? I could not imagine doing this in another's presence.

We said nothing, but walked out past old bastions of empire, Lloyds and Cooks, their massive Glasgow-made clocks with Roman numerals jostling signs in Hindi script. Also, the fountains and war memorials to the dead of the loyal dominions, ringed about with wicker baskets of coconuts, and fruit barrows manned by traders from Kerala with long knives and sarongs holding men's hips in a feminine slink.

Into Crawford Market: very dark, very high, the tall partitions hung with dusty tinware, sun pouring through the roof-lights down onto the okra and glowing aubergines, and a sweet reek of heaped mangoes and oranges, passion fruit and custard apples, and all the strange growths that go into the curry cauldron. Out into a side passage: yet more vegetables and then a clamour of goats, monkeys, tropical fish and mongrel dogs, even porcupines, fowls big and small, chickens and ducks, parrots and pigeons, the atmosphere thick with straw dust and the foetid reek of droppings pattering down from the birds onto the lids of wickers baskets from which occasionally another poor parrot would be seized and stuffed into an already bursting cage, all caught in the shafts of light streaming through the cast-iron brackets overhead. Nearby, youths played snakes and ladders on the ground.

Mid-afternoon, the Singhs' flat was empty and locked.

We killed time. Round the hill towards Malabar we walked, following small lanes and past a large private swimming pool under a copper-roofed shed where two men perched, soldering the copper, adding yet another reek to the air. Beneath us was sea and black boulders, the shit-house of the community and the laundry too, with women teetering on the rocks for one purpose or the other, large expanses of stone draped in salt-washed linens, and numbers of people howking up their dhotis near the obliging, scavenging waves. We perched on a sea wall and regarded the scummy ocean. Georgia spotted a crab wedged in a crack below us and called it 'a horrible thing with a malevolent expression'. I protested on the crab's behalf; she merely added:

'I also believe that we're in danger from snakes here. In fact I wouldn't be surprised if one climbed onto our balcony tonight.'

The Singhs' flat was still locked. What to do? Thrown back on our own resources, our companionship was thrown into uncomfortable relief. We walked up Ridge Road, home of the elite of Bombay, and ate popcorn in elaborate and fiddly public gardens full of wired-up topiary animals: lion, peacock and fox. The popcorn rustled in my inner ear. Nearby, vultures were floating over the Parsee Towers of Silence. I tipped my head back to look at them.

'They'll shit down your throat.'

'Look, though; they're dancing over the dead.'

'Free meat for birds.'

'Ought to charge entry.'

'For the meat, and for the dancing: Towers Rendezvous for vultures only, chicks must be accompanied by an adult.'

We both stood to look.

'Let's dance,' I said.

I took hold of her and attempted to waltz across the lawns between the topiary peacocks – but Georgia went cold and hard, and pushed me away.

'For God's sake, Jo, there are people watching.'

There was still so much that we could not do.

Down Nepean Sea Road, height of high fashion addresses and exclusive shops: Purple Flower, Contemporary Crafts. Grand old embassies and palatial consular residencies – turrets and terraces, wrought iron and leaded glass, peeling paint and creepers – were interspersed with towers of owner-occupied luxury. Hard by the tallest, a brute of twenty-five floors, there was a steep muddy slope smeared with the densest and most squalid collection of huts I had ever seen, a continuous greasy roof of rusting iron and wet cardboard, a crust slithering off the hill, an ulcer eating at the foot of the tower blocks, kept at bay by a high concrete wall topped with razor wire, looming over the slope. At least the rich slept horizontally.

The flat was still locked. We found a teashop and spun it out for another hour.

At 7.30 the servants appeared and let us in. We bathed off our dismay.

Then they all returned, and called for 'club sandwiches' and coffee. We sat for hours discussing the easier things, like medical reform in India, about which Dr Uttara was passionate.

I was so nearly asleep that it might as well have been a dream. All that I did... no, Georgia did it: she stretched out and hit me not very hard with the back of her wrist. This half woke me. I put out a defensive hand, and the two limbs became entangled, and we rearranged ourselves so that we lay each with an arm across the other's back, slowly coming together, surprised, alarmed and fascinated. We were neither sleeping nor awake; we lay in a shallow doze that was both genuine and bluff, nose down, trying not to breathe too hard. She twisted towards me, and for a few moments we clung onto each other until she whispered:

'Jo, go to sleep.'

I did exactly that. But I was conscious that she got up just before dawn and sat out on the balcony. A couple of hours later, when I woke, I found that she had done all our washing and had hung it up to dry.

Dr Uttara, full of bounce in spite of our chattering until all hours, called us out of our room and sat us down.

'I must talk with you.'

Mrs Singh's mother was coming to stay; and the room was needed. Dr Uttara was thoroughly embarrassed.

'I'm so sorry! I will fix something.'

She ran off to work. The servant padded in with herb omelettes.

In a gallery near the Prince of Wales Museum, a urinal was on display; it was an exhibition of Dada. Upstairs, the Gallery Chemould staff were putting last touches to a show of new works. The paintings rang a bell: there was an enormous one hanging in the entrance of the Museum of Modern Art in Delhi. Each canvas had an intense white core enclosed by concentric circles of fiercely concentrated colour. The Delhi painting had been in reds and yellows; these were in blues and purples.

We began to comment, grudging with our praise. A well-groomed gentleman with a purple shirt closed on us and enthusiastically joined in the discussion. We noted a heavy preponderance of the first person.

'I have placed the soul of art on display here. It is about force, you see?

Concentrations of overpowering force, the soul drawing the forces of the world into itself to create a unity of power, of vital energy within the artist. This is what I seek; this is what I paint.'

Standing in front of his imploding suns, this made some sense. But the artist was perhaps less confident either in his paintings or in his powers of persuasion, for he now flourished a catalogue compilation of eulogistic reviews of his work from around the world, and took us on a guided tour through these articles, pointing out the authors' names and claiming intimacy with many.

'Greenberg, now – Clement! You know Clement Greenberg? I know Clement Greenberg. He is a great man.'

He described the superb skylights of notable galleries in Amsterdam, Hamburg, Milan and Milwaukee, which brought out the special glow in his colours. I quite liked his paintings, but after half an hour of this claptrap I thought him a fraud.

'A little naive,' said Georgia under her breath, 'but let's not start making allowances.'

As we left, he thrust into our hands an invitation for tomorrow's private view.

That evening, Doctor Uttara's friend – a dashing young manufacturer – installed us in the Industrial Assurance Building, an enormous mildly art deco structure. He seemed delighted to have a pair of scruffy English parasites in his lovely new flat which he was still decorating, and in which there were no beds, but lots of sofas. He picked up the phone and rang the local Gaylord; fifteen minutes later they delivered packages of toasted ham and cheese sandwiches – the elite of India appeared to live on sandwiches – and a bag of cold fizzy drinks. He left us to roll about in baths, hooting at the toilet roll and puffing ourselves with Old Spice talc.

All day, our nervousness at re-meeting Angela had been mounting. Her train was ninety minutes late. We paced the platforms, and weighed each other in the left luggage office to the astonishment of both the staff and ourselves when we found how many pounds we'd lost. We drank milkshakes in a buffet where a Bollywood song delivered lyrics straight to the heart:

> She: *Hello darling!*
> He: *Darling darling!*
> She: *Darling darling!*
> He: *Hello darling!*

We watched the rats and the commuters, the men packed in standing while the women reclined at ease in segregated compartments, just as in *Anna Karenina*. Tacitly, we fretted at the upset of our edgy equilibrium, and wondered how we would greet Angela.

In the event, everyone did what the middle classes always do when faced with an emotional crux: we talked our heads off, chattering frantically as we sat her down in the Industrial Assurance Building. Before long, an acid note crept into the conversation, Georgia criticising all of us for accepting the hospitality of the elite, which was not India, while Angela – newly returned from the former High Commissioner's home in Sri Lanka – stared at her bemused. It became painful to listen to, Angela gently amiable and Georgia contradicting everything. And yet I knew that I would side with Georgia, and was committed.

And, after all that, Angela wasn't staying. She was broke, weepy, homesick, and determined to fly home on the first plane that Egypt Air would let her board.

'I've just re-found the calm that I lost in Nepal. Even if there was time for me to come south with you, I couldn't do it. I couldn't cope, I couldn't re-adjust yet again, not even to you two.'

I thought back to Angela in Istanbul and Herat, the gregarious mother-figure so knowledgeable about the overland trail, and how fragile she seemed here. I thought of how frantic she had once been to reach India, and how desperate to get home now. I was not sorry at all.

I scurried off to collect our own bags before the Singhs went to bed.

Dr Uttara was alone, reading peaceably. I drank lemon juice and talked a little, not daring to speak in more than a whisper. She regarded me with a gentle smile, saying little. I had no excuse for staying. I went quietly, dragging two rucksacks and sitting alone and exhilarated on the top of a bus with all the windows open, sailing along the pearl-strung seafront.

Angela and Georgia went shopping: how else would women think to make up? I walked by myself in no direction, to get away from doctors and luxury apartments.

I pottered off into the streets. A man sat in front of a portable folding booth surrounded by baskets and boxes of nuts, spices and powders. All down the lane there were identical booths. He shouted at me:

'*Gram!* Much too hot for you!'

He laughed his head off. I picked up a spiced nut and ate it.

'Mix me some, please.'

'No, no. Ha ha ha!'

'Why not? I like it.'

'No no, you cannot eat this.'

I took out my purse and asked for a small packet. He contemplated for a moment, then laughed again and began shovelling a spoonful of this, a measure of that and a pinch of other powders into a bowl on his scales, stirring it up and tipping it into a paper bag with a devious smile.

'You pay me sterling,' he said.

'Why so?'

'It is my son; he collects sterling. It makes him very happy. So you pay me a little sterling.'

In the bottom of my purse I found a ten pence coin.

'That is fine, OK, it is enough.'

He placed the coin carefully into a cigarette tin already containing five other coins and a $1 bill.

There was an interesting bamboo screen jutting a few feet into the lane. Behind it there appeared to be some sort of cafe, but with an unusual absence of signs. I poked my face round the entrance.

A toddy shop; a room full of completely silent men seated at small steel tables. They scarcely glanced at me. At the back there was a counter laden with what looked like glass milk bottles, filled with that thin, cloudy liquid you get when you rinse out a milk bottle. There were many more of these on the floor in galvanised crates, like school milk. A young boy sat on a high stool behind the bar. His voice was a monotone.

'Beer, 2 rupees. You sit down. How many bottle?'

'One.'

I sat down, and he clattered the bottle and a tumbler onto the table in front of me. It was fermented rice or palm sap or something, and it was very nasty, tasting of little but warm yeast. I sipped at it with great concentration but could barely swallow one glassful. The boy came back to my table.

'How many bottle?'

'This is enough, thank you.'

'How many bottle?'

'This is enough. Finish!'

Some of the drinkers at last looked my way, but remained quite silent. Several of the tables were well stocked with empties; I wondered how long the men had been there. I poured myself a little more, sipped, and wanted to retch. So I picked up my bottle and handed it to my nearest neighbour who nodded thoughtfully and refilled his glass as I left.

Further down the street there were stalls with signs saying 'vegetables' that sold nothing but sweets and nuts; I nibbled a tasteless lump of Turkish delight. Then I wondered what present from India might amuse my brother. There was a real wine merchant's shop in front of me.

'Do you sell Elephant Brand whisky? You know, made from bananas.'

'Ah, excuse me, my God, no, not in here, sir!'

'Oh. Do you know…?'

'Indeed, three doors down this side. Beauty Bar.'

Three doors down, between a small printers and a shop selling spare parts for ploughs, an open doorway had a sign painted on the wall:

BEAUTY BAR FOR COUNTRY LIQUORS!
1ˢᵀ FLOOR

I glimpsed a forbidding concrete tenement round a small courtyard. I dithered up the street a few yards, afraid: what would become of me in there? As I havered, a bunch of eager young men came down the street and turned briskly in. I followed them. They began to climb a steel stairway, and one of them leaned over the rail and called to me:

'Yes, come on! Beauty Bar!'

We stepped off the noisy steel stairs and entered a small room lit by a fluorescent tube. It was even starker than the toddy shop, but had the same square steel tables, and a number of young men seated in the same dedicated silence. One of the new arrivals picked up a bottle of pink hooch and sat down with a determined expression.

The light shimmered with the fumes of Elephant Brand whisky. The proprietor had been inhaling these fumes for too long; they'd gone to his legs. His speech was clear and fluent, his reasoning clear, but he had to grope his way along the walls, wobbling badly. He beckoned me into a side room stacked with crates of pink and yellow Elephant Whisky. I started bargaining, expecting to pay perhaps 15 rupees a bottle, and got two for R4.50 apiece. He seemed well pleased with this. I was about to slink out when he said loudly:

'Not to go!'

And then all the silent men burst into chorus, their glumly serious faces breaking into smiles of welcome.

'Not to go, sir! You not to go! Beauty Bar!'

The proprietor sat me down at a tin table with a complimentary glass of yellow whisky. I drank it down on top of the toddy, praying for help as my temples began to thud.

We left Angela: a quick kiss, a brisk exit in the lift, and that was that. We went to Victoria Terminus, and I felt anxiety and resentment falling away, and my pleasure in India and in Georgia returning. Out on the platforms, water pots were for sale, and the evening was full of sighing trains.

As we ate our supper in the station buffet, Georgia began speaking of some quality of 'Indian-ness' that she was still hoping to find. It sounded a strange abstraction, yet the idea seemed to move her. She said she found Delhi much more Indian than Bombay.

Out of the blue, she asked in a lowered voice:

'Would you be offended if I had been reading your diary?'

'Have you?'

She blushed very easily.

'I asked you, Jo. What would you feel?'

'I wouldn't mind, as long as you didn't get cross with me for anything uncomplimentary to yourself that you read.'

'Oh, I see, it's full of uncomplimentary remarks, is it? I thought as much from the way you smile when you're writing.'

But I was content with all the world. I smiled at her again, looked at the clock and at the train, stood and put my hand out to my rucksack.

'On we go,' I said.

214

TEN

THE PIANOS OF HYDERABAD

And thus by sleeping little and reading much the moisture of his brain was exhausted to that degree that at last he lost the use of his reason.

Don Quixote

At 9 p.m. the train left Bombay, very full, and crept north-west into the Deccan. At 2.30 in the morning at Manmad we had to change onto a narrow gauge line. The train had been waiting there for hours, and was packed. We walked across a footbridge and looked down at it.

'Did you ever see an old movie called *North West Frontier*?'

'Never heard of it.'

'It's about Indian trains full of refugees who get massacred. The trains look just like that.'

We walked slowly the length of it, weaving between large families having a midnight meal on the platform, each ringed by waiting human scavengers. At last I stopped by a window more or less at random and pushed a rucksack through. A man who had been reclining on a seat and taking up an unjust amount of space jumped up and grabbed the bag.

'Yessir, you come here, yessir!'

He bustled us onto the seat that he had been occupying, then said:

'You pay me five rupees.'

Georgia and I looked at each other. We were short on sleep, we were aggressive, and we were no longer newcomers.

'I don't think so.'

'Yes, you pay me five rupees.'

'What for?'

'For this seat. This is my own reserved seat that I am giving to you.'

'Like hell it is.'

He began to stamp his foot with rage, shouting: 'Five rupees! This is my reserved seat! Five rupees!' The other people in the solidly jammed carriage watched with interest. I was in the wrong mood for this.

215

'Piss off.'

'Five rupees!!!'

'Oh, for God's sake,' growled Georgia, 'give him one rupee and he might shut up.'

I held out one rupee.

'That's for stowing our bags.'

He looked at the coin in silent fury a moment, then climbed out of the window.

The corridors of the train were packed with beggars and the poor, squatting on the floor below window level, out of sight. But the railway police would have none of it. Four uniformed men moved down the train throwing the stowaways out while their colleagues strutted on the platform to prevent re-boarding. One ragged family dived under our seats. When a sergeant with a red and bloated face appeared, the other passengers pointed to them and the policemen dragged them out by the hair, hauled them upright and thwacked them as they scrambled off. One man, skulking behind my legs, escaped because at the critical moment there was a soft jolt on the roof and a lot of shouting and running on the part of the police. The passengers laughed:

'These people are jumping down from the bridge.'

We spent the rest of the night bolt upright. Narrow gauge trains roll much more than broad gauge; I could not sleep but could not stay awake, and began hallucinating that I was in a film production. At dawn we could glimpse the Ajanta Hills, and by 7 a.m. were eating porridge in Aurangabad. Georgia went to bed, and I sat in a tourist office wondering what to say to a pretty girl who, after consulting her timetables, insisted that a tour bus leaving the Ajanta caves at 4 p.m. would travel the fifty-odd miles back to Aurangabad with such dispatch that it arrived at 4 p.m.

To Ellora first, staggering wearily from cave to cave, from Buddha to Buddha to the more effusive Hindu temples chiselled out of the solid rock. These buildings had not been constructed but excavated, from the top working downwards: the architects had stood on a bare hillside, with a conception so clear and perfect that they could dig downwards cutting out the shape as they went. I could hardly understand this at all.

There was a group of young Indian guides walking about with books in their hands, memorising facts. One of them sat down beside me.

'Good morning to you, sir. May we have a friendship?'

I regarded him warily.

'What are you all doing?' I asked. 'There are more guides than tourists today.'

'We are all working very hard and are worried, because we are having our guiding exams tomorrow which we must pass or leave this work. So much to learn, sir, for I am also following a university course. Usually I work here only at the weekends because I also have a job in a factory. I am called Samson which is a very good name because I am strong in all my work. I love to work.'

We walked a kilometre back down the road to wait for the bus with a hundred others beneath the market tree. Women sat with baskets of vegetables, live chickens and dead chickens, all to go on the bus. Two hours later the bus could be seen approaching, streaming dust. It was obviously already full. Everyone stood up, tucking fowl under their arms...

But the driver didn't stop by the tree. He continued another hundred yards, only with great reluctance stopping to let a few people off. We ran, the women behind us sweeping up their produce and bellowing in pursuit. Not having a basket of chickens, Georgia and I just made it; no one else caught up, and there were to be no other buses that evening. I looked back at the crowd wondering what they would do now. Strap-hanging, I sang *Lord Franklin* to myself to keep awake.

> Homeward bound upon the deep,
> In my hammock and fast asleep,
> I dreamed a dream and I thought it true...

We ate at the station, the best buy in town, a splendid vegetable meal off a stainless steel platter, washed down with a cup of hot Bournvita. Georgia was very quiet, as though meditating something. We said to each other that we should get to sleep early before a long day tomorrow, and went back to our room, Georgia still oddly quiet. As we undressed and prepared for bed,

217

she suddenly put her arms about me and began kissing me passionately, caressing the back of my neck.

But no sooner had I woken up to her than she broke off as suddenly as she had begun, with a dry:

'That's enough of that.'

And went straight off to sleep.

Later, I lay awake in the dark wanting to know if it was time to get up yet. In my sleep I had been trying to visualise Angela's watch several hundred miles away. The sky told me nothing; there was no hint of dawn. So I went out walking, and found myself in Anand Vilas's tea shop where it was only 11 p.m.

Anand Vilas' Chai Shop,
Aurangabad.

They brought me four cups of nectar tea in quick succession, while starting to clean and close up. Two men worked at washing the room, each with a bucket and a plastic mug. Once dribbled water slowly over every table and stool, rubbing furiously with the ball of his hand. The other stood scrutinising the wall minutely and then, having located something on the paint that I could not see, flung his cupful of water at it as hard as he could.

The street was full of silent people. Bored blades of the town hung on the shopfront pillars. Children trickled here and there in silence, and in every doorway men slept wrapped in blankets. I sat on Anand Vilas's porch; two small girls stood in front of me staring back. We regarded each other without speaking until at last one girl stuck out her hand.

'One rupees.'

I held out a coin to show them my double-headed trick, flipping the coin rapidly so that the head appeared on both sides. The older girl took the coin, examined it, turned it over and over to find the two heads – then flung it to the ground and ran.

I'd been locked out of the hotel. I found a back door and crept in through the kitchens, but still could not sleep and sat on my bed, back to the wall, looking at Georgia's silhouette and feeling a little concerned. She had been on Imodium for three days.

Ajanta, a two-thousand year-old Buddhist monastery, is hidden in the hills a long way from anywhere. The excursion bus was full of tourists, Indians and Caucasians of all varieties. There was a middle-aged French couple in jeans cut down to shorts, bleach-streaked and embroidered with flowers. They wore solid walking boots; when I asked if they had had any good walking in India, le monsieur m'a dit que non, mon Dieu, on va en avion partout. There was an English couple of whom the wife had been brought up in India, learning to speak Hindi before learning English, this giving her a most delightful accent. The bus threaded through mud villages where women with their baskets of vegetables sat poised and ready under the tree, half-rising as the excursion bus neared, not going to be fooled again… then subsiding as we passed. At the edge of a winding gorge, the bus stopped. On the far side, in the dark grey basalt cliff, was a long row of caves.

The guide motioned us off the bus.

'Look here, please: this point is very significant for us. It is called View Point or Observation Point. From this point a British army hunting party viewed or observed these caves in 1819. For this reason, it is called View Point or Observation Point.'

I visualized the freely sweating Captain Smith out looking for meat, rising in the saddle as he noticed the dark holes opposite; my imaginary figure looked like Michael Caine in *Zulu,* in which he first appears hunting on horseback and wearing a scarlet cloak. The guide waved us down a path.

'At Cave No.1, I will begin my commentary.'

And there he set the tone:

'This cave is the most famous of these famous caves of Ajanta.'

The heat was intense, and there were steps by the hundred to climb and descend. Georgia looked weak but determined; I used my cotton sunhat to mop my face. The guide carried a powerful torch, and with this he could tug our heads to look in any direction he wished, like a puppet master. Shadows swayed and stretched amongst the carved pillars, the almost Aztec eagle forms, the stone coils and twinings among which the frescoes cowered. Everything was painted on a ground of mud mixed with rice husks, and was faded and melancholy, with cool lines and the coolest of expressions to signify rapture or despair. Even the 'Dying Princess', broken hearted at Prince Siddhartha's renunciation of the world, seemed to float three feet off the ground.

'This demonstrates the unerring mastery of the master artist,' said the guide.

In neighbouring caves the colours varied little. Afghan lapis lazuli made an appearance in one, but disappeared in the next. Another cave was half finished; the artist had moved to grander scenes next door, had left his apprentices to finishes the minor figures, and they had shirked it. Over my head, the rich abstract patterns of the ceilings seemed wildly confused until I realised that I was seeing the cracks in the rendering, thrown into sharp focus by the guide's raking lamplight. The wall portraits of the Buddha were lit at a sharp upwards angle, as though in the dark a small boy was holding a torch at his chin to scare his sister. How did the painters see all this? Did the flickering lamplight not drive them mad? If I poked my head into other chambers, silent attendants with mirrors would direct the sunlight into dark corners for me. Perhaps that was what the artists had used. I began to feel trapped, in the power of the men with lights.

The heat redoubled from cave to cave until we reached a man sitting behind three huge copper vats serving water in a shared plastic mug, 10 *paise* a time. All of us, Indian and English, French and Americans, gulped it down. We stumbled on after the guide who provided the stories and a ready reckoner of values, favourably comparing one fresco's design with Michelangelo, the atmospheric clarity of another with Canaletto. Two tourists with tripods rushed about frantically photographing everything. The guide treated them with disdain, and tweaked his flock onward with his lamp. An American asked him why the painters had used so few colours.

'This is the economic artistry.'

'Yes, but I've seen paintings older than this and they had more colours, and with the amount of paintings you have here, surely any artist would want all the colours they could get. He'd like to have the option.'

The guide looked at him seriously. It was perhaps the first interesting question he had had in months.

'These colours have been chosen to last,' he said. 'They are made from minerals which are known to last for centuries. You can see that this is true.'

Round the corner were the copyists, the Louvre-lizards with scrolls of canvas, sketching out the frescoes.

'This,' said the guide, 'is the end of the famous caves of Ajanta.'

Family at Aurangabad station, late at night. Another child asleep under the sack.

221

We sat for four hours at Aurangabad station, spinning out a pot of tea with calls for more hot water. For a while I hovered near the stationmaster's door listening to him berating a bearer for bringing him his supper cold.

'These Indians are born slaves!'

I sat on a luggage barrow and sketched a family waiting with their belongings on the platform. It was raining hard, and the station filled with beggars and banana sellers taking shelter, crowding in amongst the passengers for the Bombay and Hyderabad trains, both delayed. The local Communist Party was speeding a delegate on his way to a conference in Moscow, loading his neck with garlands, chanting slogans and making little speeches about what they expected of him, all in English.

At last the metre-gauge train swayed in out of the rain, steaming all over. A mountainous inspector dispersed the rabble besieging the couchette compartment, pulling two over-eager gentlemen off the carriage steps with all the tender politeness possible.

'Now then, you will board one at a time, please.'

Inside, he ignored the numbers on the reservation cards, and reorganised the ladies into separate bays together, announcing tremendously:

'This is not a cinema hall or a restaurant; it is a sleeper carriage where we will have no noise or disturbance, please, and you will all get some rest.'

The wooden bunks were narrow gauge too, and only five feet long. Either you curled up, or you let your feet protrude into mid-air in the corridor, making a trip to the toilet a fetishist's dream.

All night the rain deluged, the beginnings of the monsoon proper. At dawn I saw that the landscape had changed again; green and water were back, and thousands of rounded boulders.

Mrs Gupta, the wife of a family planning consultant and another of my contacts, was a wealthy woman in a Hyderabad mansion of pinkwash and verandahs, white Alsatian dogs, a dozen servants and silverware in glass cabinets. We were shown into an acre of bedroom, and Georgia promptly fell asleep again.

I sat downstairs pretending to read, but actually listening to a

222

conversation. Mrs Gupta's brother, a businessman from Madras, had colleagues in for tea. I heard familiar words but could not follow sentences at all.

'Forgive my asking, but what language are you speaking?'

'English.'

'I could understand almost nothing you said.'

'We are speaking perfectly grammatical English – but perhaps our inflexions are strange to you.'

'Do you not speak Hindi with each other?'

'Hindi? Ho, my goodness, I am a Madrasi! I speak English first, Tamil second, Hindi not at all. Never! You will forgive me – I am a fanatical southerner. Come to Madras. You have seen nothing without seeing Madras.'

'I don't think I've even seen pictures. And they don't seem to make films about south India.'

'Ah, this is because there is something in the Tamil spirit that objects to moving pictures. The Tamil is an abstract thinker, a conceptualist. He does not like his art too real. Films are not popular in the south.'

'We met a man in Fatephur Sikri,' I said, 'whose brother was a film star. He wanted Georgia to be his leading lady.'

'Hah, these people are a blight on our economy. They demand enormous salaries, half of it to be paid in undeclared black money. And where does that money come from? The two rupees, the three rupees paid by the poor man to see his favourite star.'

I remembered the cinema queue in Benares clubbed by policemen.

'In India,' he continued, 'we have cinema seats for two and a half million people, even in the villages, in school halls, mobile cinemas even. I tell you, that is where power lies in India. Forget these cities, these big factories; they will be washed aside by the small man and his hungry family who drive him to crazy, angry things. This year we have had big trouble with terrorists and Mizoram nationalists and communists. They have been assassinating politicians and landlords, and I cannot blame them one bit!'

He poured me more tea.

'You cannot imagine, you pampered young Englishman...'

I must have winced in my rotting black heart, for he leaned forward and touched my arm.

'I am sorry, I am rude, but you cannot know what the situation is for the poor man now, with landlords who treble his rent each year and send hired thugs to kill him or beat his wife and children if he protests.'

I thought of the newspaper: *Seven landless tillers fired on by landlords.*

I said: 'We saw the Aurangabad Communist Party sending a delegate off to Moscow yesterday.'

'Ah, but communism in India is far more like the rural Chinese variety than the Russian. It distresses me that we have a silly quarrel with China over a few miles of frozen Himalayan waste when our people have so many needs in common.'

Would this man feed all the poor, like Vipi on the station platform at Mughal Sarai? I risked saying:

'If you'll forgive me, this all sounds a little odd coming from a wealthy businessman.'

His friends laughed aloud.

'Listen!' said Mrs Gupta's brother, 'this country will never go communist. We have such deep sympathies with Britain; our political spirit is the same as yours. It is entirely in my interest as a businessman that the grievances in society find a voice, someone to speak up for the small man, cooperatives too. Sometimes in business I lose out – but with terrorism and chaos I stand to lose everything.'

'But the Naxalites kill landlords, not businessmen, I think?'

'Oh yes. In Germany, your European terrorists kill bankers and the public prosecutor because money and law are the gods in Germany. Our gods in India are land and statecraft, so it is landlords and politicians who get killed. But the terrorists are just a scapegoat for our own corruption. All thinking Indians know this. However, if you consider the size of India, the possibilities for violence, really we are very quiet. Suppose we were a nation of Americans, with all that grasping worldliness but reduced to a similar level of poverty – my goodness, you would see carnage then! There is, you know, a great antipathy between Indians and Americans.'

'Do you dislike Americans?'

'I have the greatest admiration for one particular American: Jon Higgins, a singer. He came here to study our southern classical music, and he achieved a great feat. He fundamentally altered his spirit, and he has become a singer of the first eminence. It is the most moving thing to hear. But he is a rarity among Americans. They all imagine themselves to be chameleons; in reality they only change as a painting changes in different lights.'

I decided not to mention my own sitar.

Mrs Gupta, his sister, was sitting smiling in the background. She had recordings of Jon Higgins, and would play them to me. She herself had a BSc but did not work, leaving that to her physician husband while she preferred to practice her religion and her arts. She played the veena, the deep-sounding sitar of the south, and had two magnificent antique instruments in a glass cabinet. She painted in half a dozen styles from Gaugin to Cubism and a little beyond. She read voraciously, she prayed hard. A room by the kitchen was given over to the family shrine, and one morning the women of the house spent hours sitting on the floor stringing tiny yellow flowers together, filling the hallways with lovely scents.

A bad mistake. A clanger. I had been misinformed. I was talking to Mrs Gupta about the population explosion in India. She said:

'Even in the last few years I have noticed, I have really felt how many more people there are in this country. You see how the trains and the buses are bursting? A bus is a metal thing, not a rubber thing. It cannot be stretched indefinitely.' (When had Mrs Gupta last been on a bus?)

'Well,' I said, 'at least your husband is in the right business, keeping the population down.'

This remark – inoffensive enough, surely, even in those times of Mrs Gandhi's sterilisation programme – produced a certain chill.

'How do you mean?' she asked.

'Well, his family planning work.'

'My husband has no family planning work.'

'Oh. Really? I thought...'

'My husband has a factory. He manufactures hand grenades.'

*

225

On September 11th, I wrote in my diary:

> Georgia has been asleep for fifteen hours. I too feel desperately tired, but I stay awake in order not to be doing quite the same thing as Georgia. For two months or more there has hardly been a day when we haven't eaten, walked, talked and slept in close proximity, even when mentally we were a thousand miles apart. We're stuck with each other, always watching each other. We've had to repress much in order to be mutually bearable. I don't know what changes might have come over me, but Georgia says I've made her much quieter.

Mrs Gupta was a fitness fanatic. I was eating breakfast alone when she came into the dining room dressed for squash.

'I play every morning. How about you?'

'Well, not every morning. But yes, I do play squash.'

'Then please come with me. I shall give you some shoes of my husband's. Are you any good?'

'Middling to mediocre.'

'I normally play with an instructor at the club, but his game begins to bore me. I think you will be more entertaining.'

I was in no condition to play squash, while the shoes were two sizes too small, and I was not prepared for a court with dirty walls and a pitch black floor. The black rubber ball simply vanished. I thrashed blindly at the air, misjudged all the angles, telescoped my toes, and began to feel sick. Mrs Gupta played like a woman bent on avenging insults.

In the Secunderabad Club showers I sat down and wept, gasping for air and clutching at my throbbing toes, laughing in spite of myself. Gentle servitors, perhaps used to this spectacle after a visit from Mrs Gupta, offered me talc and Brylcreem.

In the afternoon, the driver took us to the 16th century Golconda fort above the city, with Georgia in one of her worst moods for uncomplicated feminine reasons. It was a pleasant and desolate place of scrubby grass and massive blocks of granite oddly shaped and snugly fitted, as though built by Incas. Broad stone stairways wound up the flanks through spiked and rotting wooden gates, everything agreeably stark and curiously more welcoming as a result, where the decorations and finery of Gwalior had only emphasised its emptiness and chill. The corners of the walls jutted up and out like ships' prows. Herds of cattle grazed their way round the rocky glacis supervised by one small boy jumping from boulder to boulder. Goats postured in the ruined embrasures. In the long grass, my knees clacked against iron cannon lolling like old bull seals, and I found small, brightly painted shrines.

There was monsoon thunder threatening, and Georgia sulked and grumbled about snakes. Beyond the outworks was an army camp with tannoys bawling martial music to excite the recruits, reaching us in drifts.

At supper I still felt slightly nauseous from the exertions of squash, but attempted to put some enthusiasm into my eating. Mrs Gupta sat at the head of the table telling us that her brother and his kind were the hope of India, that private enterprise was the only possible answer in a country of such fierce individualists. I had begun to feel uncomfortable, wanting to argue, but hamstrung by her hospitality.

The food was rice, yoghurts, and cold curries. All cold, all sloppy. Mrs Gupta placed a little of each in the centre of her plate and began slowly to stir it all together with her fingertips, round and round, reducing everything to a cold grey pap. Round and round. My nausea mounted. I couldn't look in her direction.

The monsoon was washing over the city. There had been an anxious wait in the previous weeks, with public prayer meetings to end the drought. But the rain always stopped in the afternoons, so then we would go out into town.

While Georgia had a shower I enjoyed a peek at her diary, lifting open the back cover of volume one:

I looked at Jo's diary to see his reaction to the Bombay incident. Much the same as mine: confusion as to who hit who first.

227

She also found that my diary was written –

> ... as though to be read by someone else, with rather a lot rather obviously between the lines.

I had thought of it as shorthand, because my handwriting is very slow. The sound of the shower stopped; I flipped the book shut.

She was in a much better mood, and we went back to old habits, drifting aimlessly about town and sitting in a cafe near a sign saying: *Office of the Director-General of the Anti-Corruption Bureau.* We could once more remain for an hour drinking sweet tea, companions, chatting a little, drawing little sketches of nothing very much.

There seemed to be a great variety of humanity here, even more than in Delhi; I could not think why. There were the smaller, darker southerners, and gaggles of Muslims; there were even a few orthodox Jews, Africans and Chinese. I felt as alien as I had been in Kabul bazaar; the stares were of people unused to many tourists, and there were no hustlers or touts. We went cruising the town on double-decker buses, looking at exhortatory posters:

> We must fight the enemy, we must
> keep development rolling.
> Buy Government Savings Bonds!

And:

> Do your duty to your country!
> Spend less money! Save more!

And at last:

> Love may now be cheap and sensible.
> Contraceptives are 3 for 15 *paise*.

My taste for sweetmeats had returned; in particular I developed a liking for a certain green sponge, soft and soggy and tasting of angelica. One street was lined with antique and curio shops filled (said Mrs Gupta) from sales of the palaces of decayed nawabs: Chinese vases, chandeliers, worm-bored cabinets. The public had been especially indignant at reports of the entire contents of a palace being crated up and shipped off to America.

We were moving on; a car was coming to fetch us away. While we were dragging our rucksacks into the hall, a piano teacher rang the bell.

'Now, before you go,' insisted Mrs Gupta, 'I must know your opinion of this. I wish my boy to learn the piano.'

'Does he want to learn?' asked Georgia bluntly.

'That is what we are now to examine. This man will play to him and we shall see how he reacts. Vijay? Come!'

Vijay, a shy adolescent, was seated near the upright while the teacher, a diffident man in his thirties, smiled uncertainly and took out a volume of Beethoven. Mrs Gupta waved him towards the piano.

'So, there it is. Listen now, Vijay, and think whether you wish to be a musician.'

We sat and listened. The teacher either wasn't in the mood or was nervous, and his fingers went askew. His answer was to accelerate, ripping a page in his haste to reach the end of the opening allegro.

'Second movement!' he shouted, crashing energetically into a dulcet adagio. Little Vijay watched, bemused. We were saved from having to express an opinion by the arrival of the car.

Rupert was a maverick Cambridge botanist who lived in a palace by the lake. His scientific opinions were moving steadily off-centre, such that in 1981 the journal *Nature* suggested that his books should be burned as dangerous pseudoscience. In 1974, however, he was respectably employed at a plant biology research centre.

He had written to us that he lived in 'a large yellow 19th century building with lots of verandah overlooking the water.' When we had first arrived in Hyderabad, we had noticed such a place from the train.

'No,' said Georgia, clinging to the anti-elitist spirit in vogue at her Cambridge college, 'people from Clare don't live in places like that.'

But Rupert did. He rented one half of an impoverished young maharajah's home above the lake, perched on a rocky outcrop with mud huts below and decaying outhouses for the servants at the rear. He too had a piano.

'It was quite something to get hold of. There was nowhere in Hyderabad that had one for hire so I had to get it from Secunderabad, round the other side of the lake. They said they'd deliver it on the Saturday, so I stayed at home and waited. All morning people I knew kept ringing up to say: "I've just seen your piano going past. They're doing awfully well." It arrived on the heads of six men chosen for their equal height. They came jogging up the drive with the tuner trotting behind.'

He could play it; a generous stack of Bach, Beethoven and Schubert scores lay nearby. The French windows gave out onto an elegantly sculpted verandah; the cool white walls were draped with lovely paisley hangings; there were peacock feathers and cushions everywhere, Gujarati mirrored fabrics, recordings of Imrat Khan, the works of Plotinus, Hegel, Forster and Vidyapati's poems mixed with massy textbooks on plant physiology, incense, whisky and the *I Ching* on the table, and a doting manservant called Biren.

'When I first came out from Cambridge, the people at the university here gave me a room in a guest house for my first night and I went straight to bed after supper, speaking to almost no one and certainly not discussing my plans for accommodation. But word went round in the night, and in the morning there was a little queue of people squatting silently outside my bedroom door, all hoping for employment.'

The servant brought water for the whisky.

'My relationship with Biren is not unlike one's relationship with one's Cambridge bedder.'

I sat on a swing bench on the verandah peering through the dark out over the black lake at the lights of Secunderabad on the far side. The Nizam of Hyderabad's railway ran between the house and the lake shore; steam engines dragged slowly past with a snake of lighted carriages behind and the firelight glowing on the water. When Rupert returned from his shower, dressed in billowing white cottons, Biren set out the dinner: roast chicken, roast potatoes, cauliflower and gravy. Rupert said:

'It's not that I dislike Indian food. It's just that Biren has always cooked for English army families and doesn't know anything else. He wouldn't eat it himself, mind you.'

In the course of the dinner, Rupert's conversation covered the following: Indian agronomy and the failure of the green revolution; the poetry of J.H.Prynne; the slide of Asian politics into new ethnic imperialism, and the threat that this posed to the bankrupt polity of Europe; the blind alley of molecular biology as contrasted with a re-energised vitalism; memory phenomena and ghosts; Vedic conceptions of life forces and their role in the 20th century; the decadence of western culture as exemplified by its inability to reconcile Christian Humanism with mechanistic science; the value of a conflation of Western traditions with Hindu cosmic science; and a plan to save the world by increasing the ratio of male births over female.

'Male sperm swim faster than female,' said Rupert. 'All you have to do is exaggerate the difference by introducing a viscous fluid into the vagina before intercourse. Think how easy a soluble capsule of inert viscous fluid would be to produce; any small laboratory could do the work, they'd be dirt cheap and could be marketed safely anywhere. They could be sold by street peddlers for pennies. Remember that in all the countries with serious population difficulties, families are desperate for sons. In this country people spend fortunes on quacks and priests.'

'We met a couple in Fatephur Sikri who had just succeeded. They invited us to a celebratory banquet.'

'There you are. Now, consider the social consequences of this little capsule. Before two generations were out, bride-price would replace dowries. Daughters would become a valuable asset instead of a costly nuisance. I'm trying to work out how to present this to the World Health Organisation.'

At long last he rose from the cushions and stretched, saying that it was nice to have English visitors again. I asked:

'Do you miss Cambridge?'

'Good God, no. Trendy liberals are on the march in that town – not real, significant liberals, but a species of family-man academic whose height of ambition for the university is Formica-topped tables in primary colours for the senior common room. King's and Clare are unbearable these days.'

Georgia's face fell; she was rather proud of Clare.

'Where would you like us to sleep?'

'There's the big bed you're sitting on, or the cushions on the floor.'

I looked at her, and saw a momentary flash that said: Don't presume a thing. So I slept on the cushions ringed by mosquito coils. As we dozed off, she paid me a compliment:

'You know how to talk to people like Rupert. You provoke him.'

'Come off it. I was lucky to get in one sentence every three-quarters of an hour.'

'But you ask provoking questions. I wish I did.'

There was early breakfast on the verandah: fresh orange and cereals, boiled eggs, toast with marmalade of a somewhat alarming hue. After which Rupert sat at the piano and played Schubert's B flat sonata (my favourite, and difficult) with some of the finesse that little Vijay's putative teacher lacked. I stretched my arms above my head and watched the Nizam's trains curling about the lake. Then we went driving.

'If you see a Peugeot in this town, you know that the driver is an expatriate biologist.'

Out to the tombs of the Qutb Shahis, sultans of Golconda – a cluster of miniature Taj Mahals in the wilderness. The interiors were alive with swifts who made a wall-of-death spiral to reach their perches at the top, while the bubbling of pigeons echoed through the dark stink – until two teenage boys arrived with transistor radios. It was a stately pleasure garden for the dead, with potted shrubs and shaded colonnades. The Archaeology Department had decided to develop the amenities and had built a boating pond, but they had built it at the wrong time of year; there was no rain, and the cement cracked. There it was, with two rowing boats parked on the dry bottom. In the country beyond was a valley reeking of wild mint, with a small dam where buffaloes wallowed in thick mud. Small boys, entrusted with thousands of rupees on the hoof, called to each other from rock to rock. Georgia saw snakes in every cranny.

'It's a naturalist's dream,' said Rupert, 'but no one ever studies the plants or reptiles. Birds are the only wildlife that gets attention in India. There's a lot of green now, but it won't last. The whole place will dry out and curl up.'

In the distance, I saw a tiny cowering settlement.

'How does a village like that survive a drought?'

'Hardly. That's what we're working on: drought-resistant sorghums. There was near panic in Hyderabad in the last couple of weeks, before the rains began. Small children began to disappear and rumours of kidnappings started. People said the children were being sacrificed to Kali to persuade her to bring rain. Some villages lost a dozen or more, and you didn't see a single child on the streets; they were kept indoors. The more the police denied the stories, the worse the rumours.'

We all occupied separate rocks, Rupert and me on half each of an enormous boulder that had split down the middle. He meditated, while Georgia and I stared moodily at the approaching thunder.

A party: somebody's twenty-first. We collected half a dozen pals from archetypal student hovels: purple lights, loose leaf files, Hendrix posters. Then to a smart but soulless concrete blockhouse where the lamps were dim. Self-possessed girls, some in saris, some in trouser suits, even some in hot pants, snaked and swayed to progrock on the record player. There was a toxic punch of gin, rum and mango, crates of Coke, and spiced titbits. A slinky Filipino, far gone on something, sat down beside me – 'Heh, guys!' – put a hand on my shoulder and informed me that he had just had 'a damn good screw.'

Doors opened to admit the chicken curry. The Filipino instructed a pretty girl to get Rupert dancing, then sat beside me again and pointed to a girl in hot pants.

'See the cat in green pants? She's my ex-cat. Damn easy lay. She's all yours.'

Georgia was dragged off to dance while Rupert was trapped in a corner by the Filipino and a tall Nigerian engineering student who expounded their hatred of India in great detail. A motorcycle was gunned noisily outside. More of the lights were switched off, and the guys led their cats into nooks and corners. The Filipino began to stroke my hair, and I fell asleep.

Half-dozing in the back of the car, I heard Rupert tell Georgia:

'There are perhaps fifty people in all Andhra Pradesh who could behave like that, and forty-five of them were in that room.'

Another young English visitor arrived, one Steven, also from Cambridge but now come from Kathmandu where he'd been languishing in hospital with hepatitis. No sooner had we settled to breakfast than he reappeared in an orange loincloth which he claimed to have stolen from a saddhu.

We went to Sunday curry tiffin at the Secunderabad Club, amongst the colonnades and cream paint. In the Men Only bar, there were tiger skins rampaging across the panelling, yards of regimental crests, and on the posting board a list of those members who had not paid their dues and bills and had thereby forfeited the name of gentleman. In the library, the shelves were packed with neglected treasures: *The Tribes of South India Illustrated; My Fight Against Suttee; Six Years with the Assam Police*. Rupert had read most of them, and bewailed the rotting of tropical libraries.

For lunch there was mutton curry, beef curry, chicken curry, vegetable curries, vegetable cutlets, biryani rice, raita, cold cuts of beef and ham, dhal, naan and papadums, koftas and keemas, lemon cream pudding and coffee, and beer after beer – while Rupert demolished the pretensions of the Holy Spirit Association for the Unification of World Christianity's Leadership seminars, which Steven had recently attended. All the while I stared at the murals: nubile nymphs in a pallid classical landscape, painted perhaps by the Slade-trained wife of some between-the-wars staff officer.

In town, I heard a great noise coming from a temple, went to see and was swept into a hall packed with multi-coloured women all swaying with the chanting and the heat and airlessness as more and more pushed inside. I was shunted down a crudely fenced avenue into another hall where the voices and colour were twice as fierce, and my head swam. There were queues of spangled women peering over a barricade to where half a dozen fires smoked, surrounded by priests young and old, half-naked and jammed between heaps of plantains and oranges, a few chanting into microphones while the rest stoked the fires. Near the exit they were doling out handfuls of sugary cornflour granules, a leaf-fold for everyone. The press of the crowd vomited me out onto the street where I was all but washed away by a procession of transvestites and floats of Vishnite tableaux vivantes, with a flock of small boys in their wake receiving their share of the sticky granules.

I stood on top of the Charminar Gate, unable to think straight any more. Below me, the shadows of cyclists, elongated in the late sun, swept through groups of strange tribeswomen in from the country, laden with sequins and jewels in the hair, who stepped smartly away from the cycle shadows as though from death.

I was ill at last, feverish and confused. I sat on the swing bench on the verandah watching the only thing I felt I understood: the Nizam's trains. I felt scarcely able to read the last few paragraphs of *Don Quixote* – though there were only a few leaves left clinging to the cracked spine like the last tenants of a burning house, scared to jump. I regarded the valediction sadly:

> For me alone was the great Quixote born, and I for him. Deeds were his task, and to record them mine.

But I wanted to record people. It was not the Taj Mahal or the forts, the Buddhas or the ruins that I learned from: it was from a lonely

Armenian architect; from the tender courtesy of a village council; from an outspoken Madrasi businessman, and from a boy begging pennies to bury his father who may or may not have been dead; from the frantic generosity of a brass manufacturer on a train; from the baleful stare of a Sikh smuggler; from a charming young tour guide who cheated on hotel bills; from musicians, and doctors, and a wayward scientist; from hotel managers, lawyers, tubercular Nepalese, and the boys in the Beauty Bar, and all those who had felt free to comment on the state of my soul. And it was from Georgia, and her powers of observation, synthesis and tolerance. Never from monuments, and never from vapid abstract notions of the East.

It was Georgia who investigated the night train to Bombay. She examined a railway timetable which said that it departed at 8 p.m. To be sure, she rang two separate enquiry offices. One said it left at 7.30, the other said at 9.00. Georgia grinned and declared that departure was all a state of mind.

Bombay again. Was it the delusion of a battered brain? I was sure that I had reserved a Railway Retiring room at Bombay Central, that I did write our names and the date required in some great brown register, but they had no record of it. So we found ourselves in the Connaught Hotel, a hot, windowless and shabby dive. Today the name belongs to a 4-star luxury establishment: not in 1974. It was close to the priceless plush of the Taj Mahal Hotel, but I could not have afforded to urinate there.

We unpacked and considered our collections, spreading them on the steel cots, staring in incomprehension at objects which we must have purchased but could not understand why: ugly rings from Kabul, a bottle of Iranian Milk of Magnesia, and a heap of other unwanted medicines.

Here in the Connaught Hotel were the young travellers again, as though gathered to say goodbye but with memories too blurred. I went from room to room asking if anyone wanted a supply of plasters, Imodium and antiseptic cream.

'Weren't you at Sigi's in Kabul?'

'No. I don't think so.'

236

We took our bags to the station to weigh them. Georgia panicked, momentarily mistaking pounds for kilos.

'Oh God, Jo, it's impossible, it's a bloody disaster.'

'For Christ's fucking sake, calm down, will you?'

We looked at each other in shock – and laughed. On the way back to the hotel a smartly dressed young man stopped me in the street and offered me a job as a film extra.

That evening, in our windowless, airless, neon-lit room, we sat on our steel cots, undressed and, without saying anything, reached out for one another, as though this was the conclusion of a pact made in Istanbul months before, and quietly nurtured all the way between.

We took a train out to the airport. As it paused somewhere, I looked out and saw in the street below the line a cafe.

It was rush hour, and Georgia was fainting with the heat, standing packed against the door by perspiring bodies. I thought both she and my sitar in its sleeping bag would be crushed at any moment. But a small, elderly teacher of dance came to our rescue, calling on his neighbours to form a protective barrier around Georgia and the instrument. These kind people got us off the train in one piece, and the dance teacher bought us each an iced Coke to revive us. Such perfect, casual kindness.

At Santacruz airport, Georgia slept on the bench beside me, covered against the evening chill in a cheap and very coarse horsehair blanket I had bought, which today is folded over the back of my sofa. Our flight was delayed by three hours. The Egypt Air desk informed me that by some muddle our seats from Cairo to London had not been confirmed after all, that there was no other flight to London before next weekend, and that they would pay nothing towards accommodating us in Cairo. We had no money left. I looked at Georgia sleeping, and wondered how I would ever find the nerve to tell her.

*

'I like this well enough,' said the curate, 'yet, after all, I cannot persuade myself that there is anything of truth in it. However, I must confess I have nothing to object against his manner of telling it.'

Don Quixote